KEY STAGE THREE

EDUCATIONAL

NATIONAL CURRICULUM

GEOGRAPHY

Mike Clinch

Adviser's comments: David Waugh

First published 1992

Editorial team
Andrew Thraves, Rachel Grant, Angela Royal

Design team
Jonathan Barnard, Keith Anderson, Peter Holroyd

Text © Mike Clinch 1992

Illustrations: Ian Foulis Associates, Chris Evans

© BPP (Letts Educational) Ltd
Aldine House, Aldine Place
142–144 Uxbridge Road
London W12 8AW

Printed and bound in Great Britain by
WM Print Limited, Walsall, West Midlands WS2 9NE

**British Library Cataloguing in
Publication Data**
Clinch, Mike
Key Stage 3.
Geography.
I. Title
910

ISBN 1 85758 111 3

Acknowledgements
Thanks go to David Bell, David Waugh and
Peter Goddard, the advisers on this book.

The author and publishers are grateful to the following for permission to
reproduce photographs and prints (page numbers refer to this book
unless stated):

Aerofilms Ltd p100, 127; Allsport Picture Library (David Cannon) p31;
The Channel Tunnel Group Limited p136; Bruce Coleman Limited pp18,
31, 33, 34, 35, 36, 37, 40, 41, 44, 56, 70, 75, 81, 85, 88, 91, 94,
95, 96, 98, 107, 113, 115, 116, 117, 128, 129, 132, 144, 148,
159, 163, 164, 168, 128, 144; The Cheltenham Newspaper Co Ltd
p76; DIAF Agence D'Illustration Photographique pp34, 35, 37; The
Environmental Picture Library: p51 (Shahidul Alam/Drik/CARE) p85
(A Greig), p85 (V Miles), p85 (Micheal McKinnon), p148 (J Holmes),
p161 (Paul Glendell), p164 (Heidi Bradner); Frank Lane Picture Agency
Ltd pp67, 68, 69, 70, 71, 102, 111, 114; Geoscience Features Picture
Library p89; Holt Studios International pp60, 76, 148, 166; The Italian
State Tourist Office (ENIT) London pp31, 69; Marion and Tony Morrison
pp56, 58, 60; The National Meteorological Library p107, 108;
Ordnance Survey map extracts reproduced with the permission of the
Controller of Her Majesty's Stationery Office © Crown Copyright pp13,
20, 77, 91, 100, 132; Oxfam Photo Library p145; Quadrant Picture
Library p145; QA Photos p145; Science Photo Library pp67, 111, 151;
Somerset County Gazette p133; Tony Stone Photolibrary, London pp26,
32, 40, 51, 107, 163; Ian Thraves Photography pp40, 81, 87, 88, 91,
92, 93, 94, 96, 98, 129, 134, 141, 142, 152, 151, 153, 159, 160;
Topham Picture Source pp53, 86, 123, 163; Tony Waltham Geophotos
p51, 92, 93, 94, 96, 98, ; J Wildgoose c 1990 p101; Woodmansterne
Picture Library, Photos © WOODMANSTERNE pp91, 132.

Grateful acknowledgement is also due to Exmoor National Park Authority
and to B T Batsford Ltd

CONTENTS

ABOUT THE NATIONAL CURRICULUM

As you complete the activities in this book and make progress through school, you will be following the National Curriculum. All pupils of your age across the country will be doing the same subjects.

The National Curriculum consists of 10 subjects which you must study at school. These are divided into core and foundation subjects.

English, mathematics and science are the core subjects. They will help you study all the other subjects. The other subjects are the foundation subjects. Although it is not part of the National Curriculum, you will also study religious education at school.

KEY STAGES

You are now at Key Stage 3 (which goes from age 11 to age 14). It is one of the four Key Stages which you go through as you complete your education to age 16. The four Key Stages are:

Key Stage 1: ages 5 – 7

Key Stage 2: ages 7 – 11

Key Stage 3: ages 11 – 14

Key Stage 4: ages 14 – 16

ATTAINMENT TARGETS

Each subject has its own objectives or goals. These are called Attainment Targets and explain what you are expected to be able to do. Each Attainment Target has 10 levels and you will progress through one level at a time. The average 14-year-old will achieve level 5 or 6 depending on the subject but you might do better than this in a particular subject.

TESTING AT AGE 14

When you are 14 and have completed Key Stage 3 you will be given a series of tests, not set by your teacher, but one taken by all 14-year-olds across the country. These tests will measure the standard that you have reached.

PROGRAMME OF STUDY

Each subject also has a programme of study. This describes the work you have to do to meet the Attainment Targets. This book provides practice in the work that makes up the Programme of Study in geography. By completing the activities in the book, you will be much better prepared for the tests at age 14.

GEOGRAPHY IN THE NATIONAL CURRICULUM

At Key Stage 3 in geography, you are expected to make progress in five Attainment Targets (AT):

AT1: Geographical skills

AT2: Knowledge and understanding of places

AT3: Physical geography

AT4: Human geography

AT5: Environmental geography

So, what kinds of things will you be doing as you cover Key Stage 3 geography? You will learn the skills of the geographer, such as making accurate measurements of geographical features and conditions, extracting information from maps and identifying and describing geographical patterns. In particular, you will make detailed observations of the weather, follow a route using an Ordnance Survey map, make and use your own short maps and interpret all kinds of other maps. When you look at places, you will be focusing on the part of the country in which you live. You will also look at European countries such as France or Italy, an economically developing country such as Bangladesh or Brazil, and make a comparative study of the USA, Japan and the Russian Commonwealth.

Physical geography concentrates on the main features of the Earth such as river systems, temperatures, weather, volcanoes and earthquakes. But geography is also about people and at Key Stage 3 you will look at population changes, economic development, transport and settlements. You will explore why people make the decisions they do about where they live and work. You will also examine the particular features of villages, towns and cities.

Finally, environmental geography will allow you to explore many issues of topical interest such as the use of natural resources, the effects on the environment of using different kinds of energy sources such as coal and gas, and the ways in which people can both destroy and improve the environment.

Don't be too worried if some of these subjects are unfamiliar to you at the moment. The National Curriculum is designed to develop your understanding as you progress through the different levels in each Attainment Target. This book will help you to do well.

Good luck and enjoy National Curriculum geography!

INTRODUCTION

This book has been written to help you in your studies for National Curriculum geography, Key Stage 3, and is based on the five geography Attainment Targets.

It is not intended to be a scheme of work. The book's content is laid out in the same order as the National Curriculum so all work associated with Attainment Target 1 comes at the beginning, followed by all work associated with Attainment Target 2, and so on. The exception is Attainment Target 5, environmental geography, which, due to the nature of its content, has been integrated where appropriate. You should, therefore, use each unit where necessary to support school-based work. By doing this you will gain a wider perspective and a deeper understanding of key geography topics.

Each unit of the book is made up of explanatory text and a series of activities. These activities are found in Action! boxes. You should read through the relevant section of text before attempting these activities. The answers to most of the Action! exercises will be found at the back of the book. The exceptions are those activities which are locally based, as there is a large and unpredictable range of possible answers.

Fieldwork is an integral part of National Curriculum geography and some suggestions for fieldwork topics and project-based work have been included at various points in the text. You will find these under the heading Fieldwork/enquiry.

It is hoped that parents will also feel encouraged to read through this book so that they can get a better idea of what modern-day geography is all about, and so be able to help their children at any stage.

I would like to thank Peter Nash and his daughter, Emily; Rachel Jones, Stephen Cameron, Denis Meadmore of Coed Morgan Farm and the staff of the NRA (Monmouth) for their contributions. I would also like to thank Angela Royal and Andrew Thraves for giving me the opportunity to write this book. I am especially grateful to Andrew for his support, patience and confidence during the project.

I am particularly indebted to my wife, Charmaine, for her help and guidance. Without her this book would not have been possible.

Mike Clinch

UNIT 1
Basic skills

THE BRITISH ISLES POLITICAL: COUNTRIES AND CITIES

The British Isles is made up of five countries – England, Scotland, Wales, Northern Ireland and the Republic of Ireland (Eire). Each of these countries has its own capital city although only one, Eire, has its own separate government.

An atlas displays two kinds of maps. **Political maps** show countries, cities, main roads and other 'human features'.

Physical maps show mountains and rivers and other 'natural features'.

Letter–number co-ordinates are used on some maps to find places more accurately. For example on the map opposite co-ordinate A1 is clearly marked.

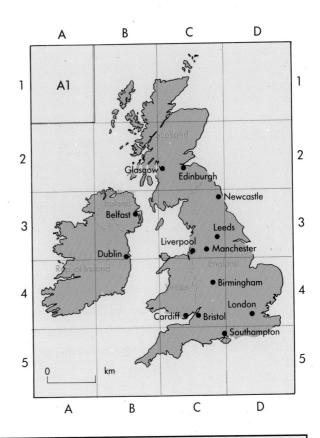

ACTION!

Look at the map above.

1 Name the cities at each of these co-ordinates:

(a) D4 (b) C5 (c) B3

2 Give the co-ordinates for:

(a) Newcastle (b) Liverpool (c) Cardiff

3 Which co-ordinate has the most number of cities?

Answer these questions using the compass opposite and the map above.

4 Leeds is south of_____.

5 Glasgow is _____ of Edinburgh.

6 Birmingham is north-east of _____.

7 Cardiff is _____ of Dublin and west of _____

8 _____is south-east of _____ and south of _____.

9 Using a political map of Britain in an atlas, locate approximately where you live.

10 Describe your location using the words country, region, county and town.

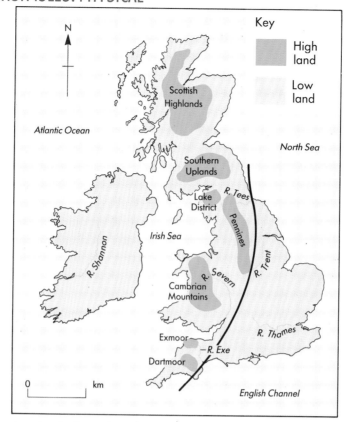

Britain can be divided into highland Britain and lowland Britain by a line joining the mouth of the River Exe in Devon with the mouth of the River Tees in Cleveland.

To the north and west of this line the rocks are old, very hard and therefore form mountains. To the south and east of the line the rocks are much younger, softer and have therefore been eroded into lowlands.

Rivers

All rivers begin their lives as small streams flowing out of the mountains or as springs. As they flow downhill they gradually get larger as more streams join together. Eventually, rivers will end where they flow into a larger river *or* where they flow into the sea. Words associated with rivers include:

Source   where a river begins

Course   the path and direction a river takes

Channel   the wet area between the banks of a river

Tributary   a small river flowing into a larger one

Mouth   where a river ends

ACTION!

Find a physical map of the British Isles in an atlas or look at the illustration above to help you complete the table below.

River	Source	Mouth
Trent	Southern Pennines	
Thames		
	Exmoor	
		Bristol Channel
Tees		
		Atlantic Ocean

WHAT IS A MAP?

However we choose to find out about an area it is highly likely that we would use a map at some stage. Maps are used by all types of people in their jobs – e.g. travel agents, estate agents, taxi drivers – and also in their leisure time e.g. ramblers, hikers, tourists. There are many different types of map. There are street maps, road and Ordnance Survey maps, to name just three. Some, like O.S. maps, are very detailed; others, like sketch maps, give only brief information about an area.

Sketch maps

A sketch map is the least accurate type of map because it only gives a rough idea of the distance between places. Sketch maps can be used to give someone directions when planning a route. The illustration below is an example of a sketch map.

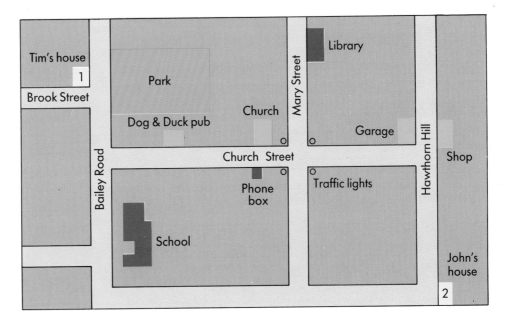

ACTION!

Tim intends to visit his friend John after school. He has to go home first to tell his parents where he is going and then return a library book before going on to John's house.

Describe Tim's route from school to John's house.

Plans

A plan is a drawing of something as seen from directly overhead. Plans may be used to give a bird's-eye view of buildings, parks, shopping centres, etc. The illustration overleaf shows a plan of a school.

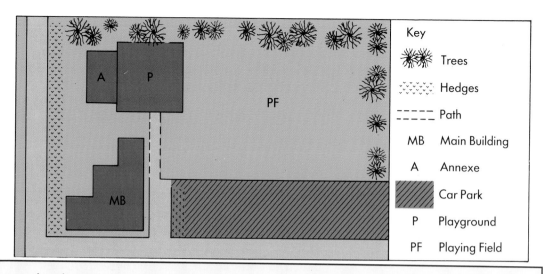

ACTION!

Your local newspaper is running a competition to design the layout for a new park in your community. The rules of the competition state that the park must include the following facilities:

children's playground   adventure playground   duck pond   ornamental gardens and fountains   ice cream kiosks   paddling pool   picnic area   tennis courts   playing field toilets and first aid station

Draw your competition entry using appropriate symbols and labels for your layout.

Ordnance Survey maps

Maps produced by the Ordnance Survey show areas of the UK in great detail. Special skills are needed to be able to read and interpret them accurately.

Map symbols

It is not possible to label every feature included on a map. For this reason, signs and symbols are used to represent the various features we want to include on a map, which are then explained in a key. The symbols can be lines, small drawings, letters or coloured areas. Listed below are some of the symbols used on OS maps of the 1:50 000 series.

Lines	**Small drawings**	**Coloured areas**	**Letters**
M 1 — Motorway	⟶‖⟵ Bridge	National Trust (open) NT	P Post office
A 40 — Main road	⌐ Golf course	(closed) NT	PH Public house
— Secondary road	♦ ♦ + Three types of church	Wood	MP. Mile post
— Railway	⊘ Glasshouse	Park	CH Club house
— Railway:single track	⁚⁚ Tumulus	Orchard	TH Town hall
●━■ Railway stations	Triangulation pillar	Quarry	
～ Viaduct		Buildings	
◁▥▷ Cutting	Ⴘ Windmill	Lake	**Tourist information**
⫶⫶⫶ Embankment	ⵏ Windpump	Beach	
◁▥▷ Tunnel	⬤ Coach station	Sand — (sand) Shingle (shingle)	ⓘ Information centre
⋯⋯ Footpath	Ⲛ Lighthouse		Ⓟ Parking
National park boundary	ⵕ Beacon	Cliffs	✕ Picnic site
River	⌢ Battlefield	Spoil heap	☀ Viewpoint
> ‑ ‑> ‑ ‑> Pipeline	27 Spot heights		Å Campsite
×—×—× Pylons			⌂ Caravan site
≋≋ Contours			▲ Youth hostel

Scale and Distance

One of the most important uses for a map is to show how far one place is from another. Scale allows us to do this.

The amount of detail shown on a map is also determined by the scale. A large scale map shows a small area in great detail. A small scale map shows a large area in less detail. If you wanted to find information about a village then a large scale map would be most useful, whereas if you wanted to find information about a country, then it is better to use a small scale map. Scale can be expressed in three ways:

As a linear (line) scale

e.g. 0 |___|___|___|___| 1 km

As a statement

e.g. 4cm = 1km

As a ratio

e.g. 1:25 000

The three maps below show the same area on three different scales.

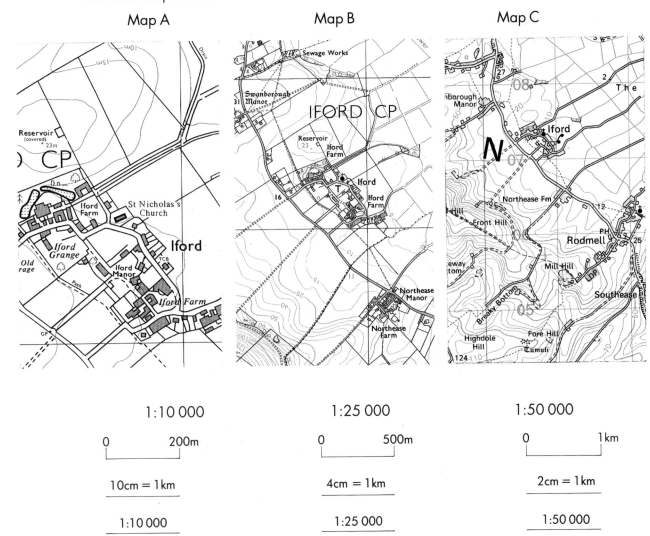

| Map A | Map B | Map C |

1:10 000	1:25 000	1:50 000
0 200m	0 500m	0 1km
10cm = 1km	4cm = 1km	2cm = 1km
1:10 000	1:25 000	1:50 000

How to measure distances

Look at map B above.

If the scale is 4cm=1km then this means that every 4cm measured on the map represents 1km on the ground.

Example: a line measuring 6cm:

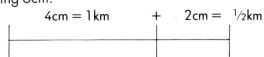

4cm = 1km   +   2cm = ½km

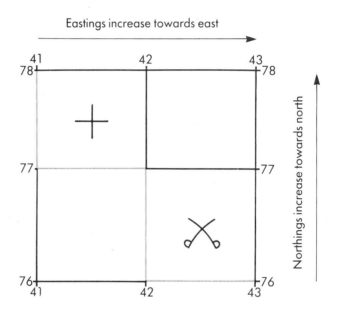

ACTION!

Measure the distances on the ground which these lines would represent. Look at the scale very carefully. Remember that scale can be written in three different ways.

Scale		
4cm = 1km	(a)	———————————————————
	(b)	—————————————————
	(c)	———————
1:50 000	(d)	——————————————————————
	(e)	—————————
	(f)	————————————————
0 100m	(g)	———————————————
	(h)	——————————
	(i)	—————————

Grid references

Four figure grid references

To find places accurately, OS maps have a grid drawn on them. The grid is made up of a series of lines going up and down as well as across the page. Each line has a number written at its end.

Vertical lines are called **eastings** – numbers increase towards the east. Horizontal lines are called **northings** – numbers increase towards the north.

The two lines that cross in the bottom left hand corner (south-west) make up the unique grid reference for that square.

For example the four-figure grid reference for:

The church (+) = 4177

The battlefield (✕) = 4276

When reading grid references always remember **an L shape** and to **write eastings before northings.**

14

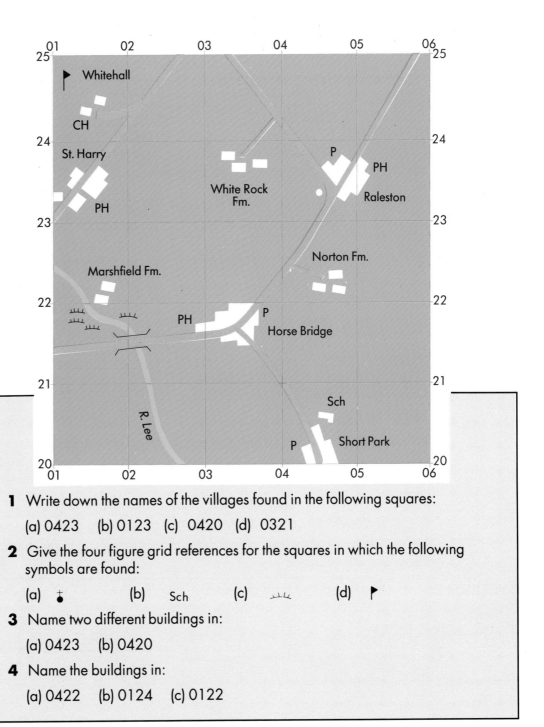

1 Write down the names of the villages found in the following squares:

(a) 0423   (b) 0123   (c) 0420   (d) 0321

2 Give the four figure grid references for the squares in which the following symbols are found:

(a) ☨   (b) Sch   (c) ⊥⊥⊥   (d) ▶

3 Name two different buildings in:

(a) 0423   (b) 0420

4 Name the buildings in:

(a) 0422   (b) 0124   (c) 0122

Six figure grid references

A four figure grid reference is useful when finding a particular square on a grid. On OS maps of 1:50 000 and 1:25 000 series a grid square represents the square kilometre. Sometimes greater accuracy than this is required when locating a specific point such as a building or map symbol, in which case we use a six figure grid reference, which is accurate to within 100 square metres. For example, in the diagram, to give the six figure grid reference for the youth hostel in square 4176:

(a) read existing line 41 + two parts of the way towards line 42, so the first three numbers are 412;

(b) read northing line 76 + three parts of the way towards line 77, so the next three numbers are 763;

(c) therefore, the six figure grid reference is 412763.

The six figure reference for the bus station is 425776.

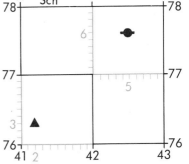

Use the map to complete the table.

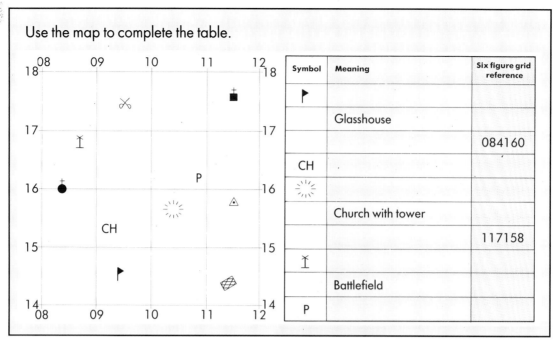

Symbol	Meaning	Six figure grid reference
⚑		
	Glasshouse	
		084160
CH		
☼		
	Church with tower	
		117158
⚲		
	Battlefield	
P		

Height on maps

The land around us is not flat like a piece of paper. So when a map is drawn, various methods are used to show the different heights of the land. These methods can tell us exactly how high a mountain is as well as giving us an idea about the **relief** (shape of the land).

On a map, height may be shown in three ways:

Using colour or shading In the diagram that follows, different heights are shown by different bands of colour.

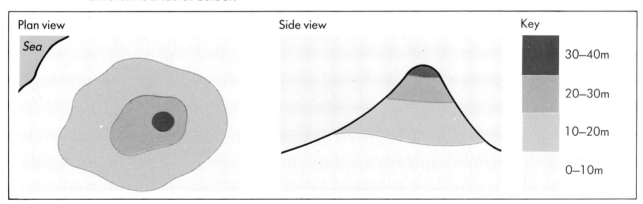

Spot heights These are dots on the map with a number next to them. The number indicates exactly the height of that point above sea level.

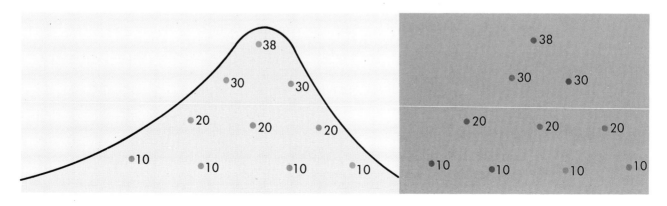

Contours Contours are lines joining places of the same height above sea level.

For example:

30
20
10
Higher land

Everywhere along the contour line marked 10 is 10 metres above sea level. Contour lines never cross each other.

ACTION!

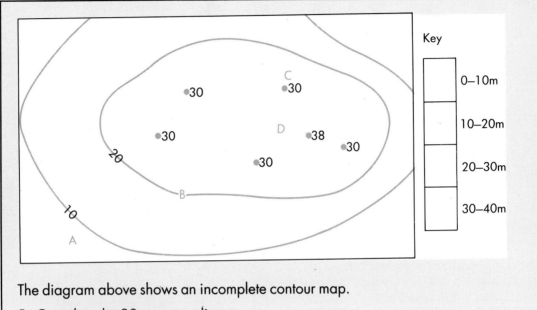

The diagram above shows an incomplete contour map.

1 Complete the 30m contour line.

2 Give the heights of the points marked A, B, C and D.

3 Using a graded scale shade the map according to height and complete the key.

Using contour lines

In order to get a better idea of the shape of the land shown on an OS map it is necessary to look carefully at the contour lines. Each contour line represents a change in height. The space between each line shows the distance on the land you would have to travel in order to gain 10 metres in height.

When contour lines are close together the land is steeply sloping; when they are far apart, the land is gently sloping. If there are no contour lines then the land is flat.

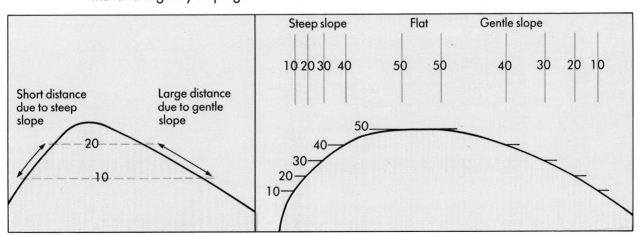

Contour patterns

Groups of contour lines drawn together make up a contour pattern. Contour patterns show the shape of the land and common landscape features have their own distinctive contour patterns. There are as many contour patterns as there are landscape features. Four such patterns have been outlined below. (Take special note of the height of each contour.)

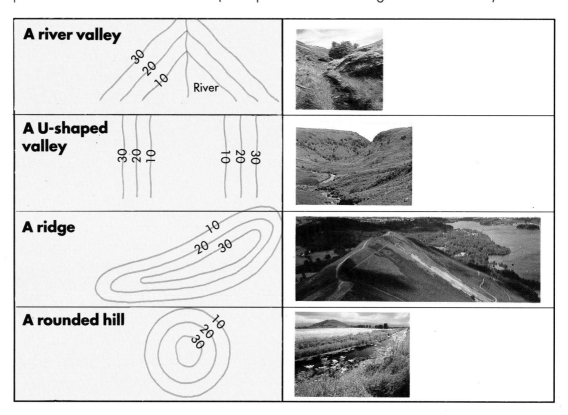

A river valley

A U-shaped valley

A ridge

A rounded hill

Drawing cross-sections

The best way to get a more accurate picture of the shape of the land using contour lines is to draw a **cross-section**. The contour lines on a map give the overhead view – when you draw a cross-section it's as if you are looking at the land from the side, so that you can see an outline showing the shape of the land between two given points.

There are two methods of drawing a cross-section:

Method 1

1 Using a ruler, draw a line between two points A and B. This is your **line of section**.

2 Draw a frame below the contour map. It should be exactly the same width as the line A-B.

3 The vertical scale should go from 0 to above the value of the higher contour.

4 Each time the line of section crosses a contour, draw a faint line down to the frame as far as the value of the contour and mark the point with a cross.

5 When all the crosses have been marked onto the frame, join them up with a smooth curve (do not use a ruler) to show the outline of the land.

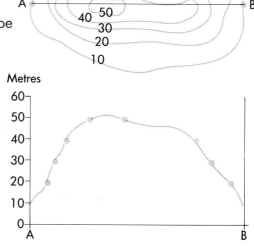

It may not always be possible to draw a cross-section in this way if there is not enough room beneath the contour map, or particularly if you want to transfer information from a map into your workbook.

Method 2

1 Using a ruler, mark on the map the line of section A-B.

2 Take a piece of paper and lay the edge along the line of section. Mark points A and B onto the paper.

3 Each time the line of section crosses a contour mark it onto the paper and note the height.

4 Draw a frame on which to draw the cross-section as in steps 2 and 3 above.

5 Place the piece of paper along the base of the frame and transfer the points and heights onto the base line.

6 Draw the faint lines upwards from the baseline and mark the points with a cross at the correct heights.

7 Join up the points with a smooth curve.

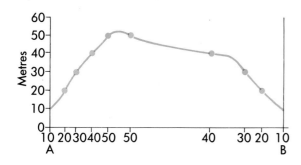

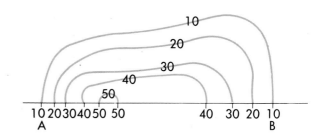

ACTION!

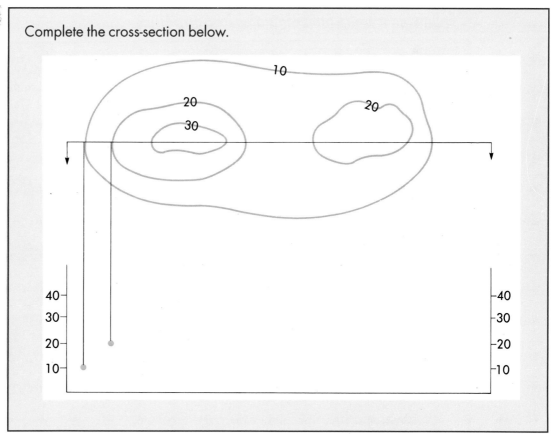

Complete the cross-section below.

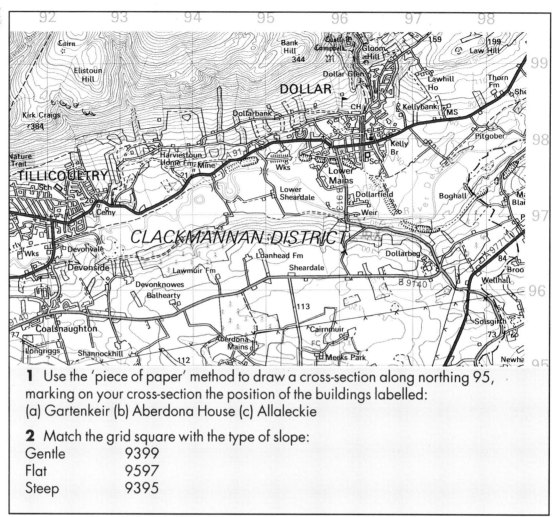

1 Use the 'piece of paper' method to draw a cross-section along northing 95, marking on your cross-section the position of the buildings labelled:
(a) Gartenkeir (b) Aberdona House (c) Allaleckie

2 Match the grid square with the type of slope:

Gentle	9399
Flat	9597
Steep	9395

Following a route on a map: the Treasure Hunt

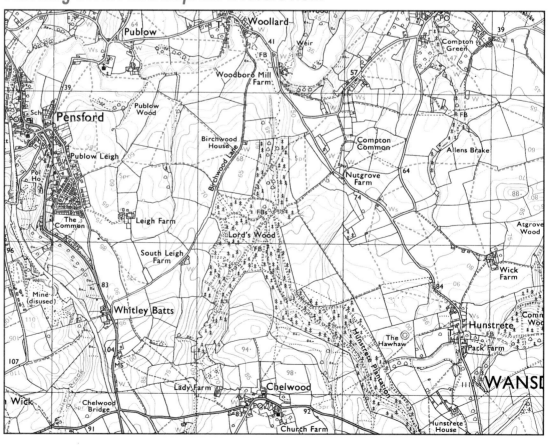

The idea of a treasure hunt is to follow a route on a map, picking up the answers to questions on the way.

1 Find the school in Pensford. Follow the main road south from the school.
  (a) How high is the first spot height you see?
  (b) Name the first hamlet you pass through.
  (c) Name the bridge at the crossroads.

2 Turn left at the crossroads.
  (a) In which direction are you now travelling?
  (b) Name two buildings in Chelwood.

3 Follow the road and take the first turning north.
  (a) Name the first farm you pass through.
  (b) Name the area of woodland you can see to your left.

4 Follow the road as far as Wollard. Turn west just after the bridge.
  (a) For the first ½ km, are you travelling uphill or downhill?
  (b) To see the river would you have to look north or south?

5 Follow the road over the bridge.
  What is the first spot height you pass?

6 You want to get back to the school as quickly as possible.
  (a) At the junction do you:
    (i) turn right and right again;
    (ii) turn right and then left;
    (iii) go straight on?
  (b) If you have taken the shortest route, how far do you think you have travelled – about 5km, 10km, 15km or 20km?

USING GRAPHS

When we are working with facts and figures we can use graphs to show the information in a clear and direct way. We can also learn a lot of information by studying the shapes of graphs carefully. There are four main types of graph and it is important to choose the right kind to clearly show the information.

Line graphs are used to show **averages** and how things change over time. The **steeper** the graph the **greater** the change. If the graph is **flat** then there is no change over time.

Example:
the average temperature

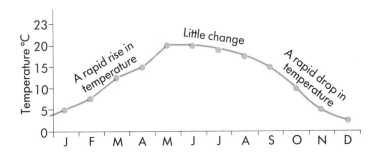

Bar graphs are used to show totals. The longer the 'bar' the greater the total.

Example: total rainfall for each month of the year

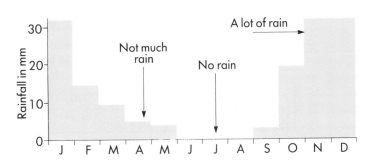

Pie graphs are used to show percentages. The 360° in a circle equal 100%, so every 1% = 3.6 of the circle.

Pie graph to show the percentage of land used on a farm

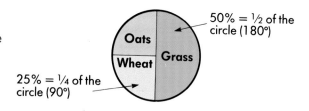

50% = ½ of the circle (180°)

25% = ¼ of the circle (90°)

Scattergraphs are used to show relationships. What happens to one thing as the other changes?

For example: rainfall and water in a river

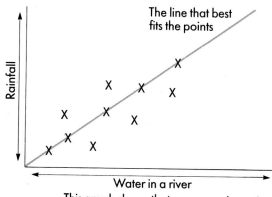

The line that best fits the points

This graph shows that as more rain falls, the amount of water in the river also increases

ACTION!

Draw a graph for each of the four sets of figures outlined below. Choose the most appropriate forms of graph for each.

1 Percentages to show how people travel to work in a city centre office

Car	50%
Bus	20%
Train	25%
Walk	5%

2 The relationship between the number of cars in a city centre and the levels of pollution

Number of cars	Pollution
100	Very low
200	Low
500	Average
1000	High
1500	Very high

3 The total number of vehicles travelling down a main street in a day

am	Midnight	1	2	3	4	5	6	7	8	9	10	11	Noon
	20		15	5	3	5	10	20	50	140	120	100	70	80

pm	1	2	3	4	5	6	7	8	9	10	11	Midnight
	120	100	80	130	130	100	80	50	60	30	25	20

4 The total number of visitors to a tourist centre during each month of the year

J	F	M	A	M	J	J	A	S	O	N	D
20	15	40	100	500	1000	1100	1200	600	400	80	40

UNIT 2
The local area

WHERE DO I LIVE?

The places in which people live all have names. The name of a place makes it easier to find on a map and can show where that location is in relation to other places. Every house or flat has an address which tells us exactly where that house or flat is located and enables the postman/woman to deliver letters and parcels to the correct place.

- Put your name, house number and street in the address table.
- Your street may be part of a larger area which in turn is part of a town.
  (If you live in a small town or village then you may not have a district.)
- All towns are in a county. In which county do you live?
- Name the country in which you live.

My address

Name _____

Number/Street _____

Larger area _____

Town _____

County _____

Postcode _____

Country _____

Taking a closer look at a street

Case study: Stephen's street

Stephen lives in a small street in the village of Trelewis near Merthyr Tydfil in Mid Glamorgan, South Wales. Here is a plan of his street.

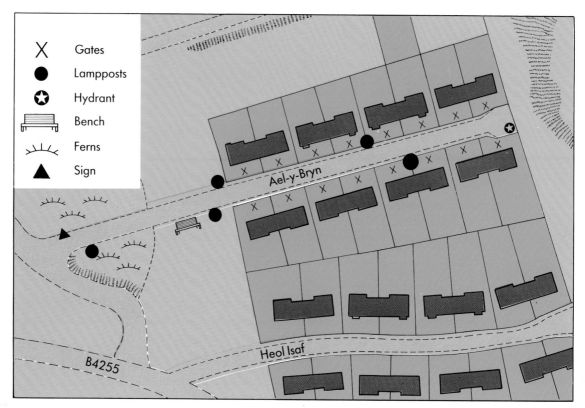

Legend:
- X — Gates
- ● — Lampposts
- ✪ — Hydrant
- 🪑 — Bench
- ⤜ — Ferns
- ▲ — Sign

(Map labels: Ael-y-Bryn, Heol Isaf, B4255)

ACTION!

Look at the plan above.

1 How many houses are there in Stephen's street?

2 What is the name of his street?

3 Stephen's street is a dead end. Do you think there will be a lot of traffic? Who would use his street?

4 Draw a sketch map of your street, or if you live in a long street, just draw the section around where you live. Don't forget to add any lampposts, public telephones and other features.

ACTION!

Fieldwork/ enquiry

Use the questionnaire outlined below to find out more about your street. Try to ask as many of your neighbours as you can. (Remember – always be polite when asking people questions.)

1 Name and address of person interviewed.

2 How long have you lived here?

3 Do you know how the street got its name?

4 Has anything changed in the street since you moved here?

5 Are there any improvements you would like to see in the street?

YOUR LOCAL AREA

Your street is just a part of your local area. It is useful to know what the environment around us is like, and it is important to know where to find certain places.

Questions to ask ourselves about our local area could include:

- Where is the nearest bus stop or railway station?
- What is the way to school?
- Where is the nearest park or youth club?
- How far is it to my best friend's house?
- Which way are the shops?
- Can I walk to the local sports centre, or is it too far?

ACTION!

'I go out of school and turn left. I walk along Coronation Street and I can see some swings on my left. To my right is the park, with trees and a duck pond in it. Next I turn left into Ramsey Street and I can see the shop on my right. I walk past my neighbour's house and I am home.'

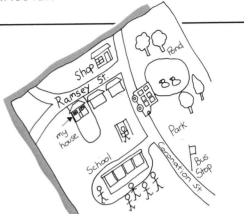

Take a look at the streets where you live. Make a note of the places or buildings you could put on a map. Don't forget your own house.

1 Draw a rough map first and then when you are happy with it make a neat copy. Colour in your map.

2 Describe in words a route you would take from your house to one of the buildings you have drawn.

IN WHICH REGION DO YOU LIVE?

The United Kingdom can be divided into a number of regions. A region is a large area of the country, made up of a number of counties. Usually there is one large city in each

Regions of the British Isles

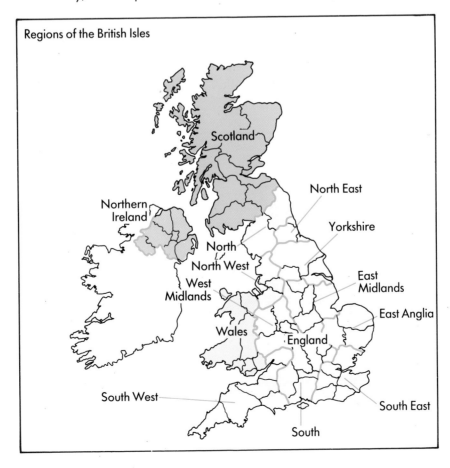

25

region, but larger regions can have more than one city and many large towns. Sometimes there are no definite boundaries to regions. One person's ideas of what that region is can be different from their neighbour's. So, general terms such as south-east, or east Midlands, are used to describe regions.

ACTION!

How to find out the name of the region in which you live.

1 What is the name of your local:
(a) Electricity Board (b) Gas Company (c) Water Company (d) TV station?

2 In which county do you live?

3 Using the map on page 25, name the counties which surround your county.

4 Name the region in which you live.

Images of different home regions

Local areas within regions can vary enormously. Some of us live in the countryside, some in a town. Some of us live in large cities. Some people live on modern housing estates – others live in older houses in old industrial regions.

What is it like to live in the country?

I live on a farm of about 60 acres. The nearest village is about a mile away, but there are no people of my age living there

I like living in the countryside because I like plenty of open spaces. I like to walk and I like being away from the noise and pollution of towns

It takes me about 45 minutes to get to school. I have to catch two different buses

I do get out quite a bit though. The local town has a cinema and sports centre, but I have to have a lift to get there

There are quite a lot of things I don't like about the countryside. I don't see my friends much after school, as they live in towns

When I'm older I'd like to live out in the country, but within easy reach of a big town

I have to rely on my parents to take me everywhere. Sometimes they can't because they are very busy on the farm

ACTION!

1 What does Rachel **like** about living in the countryside?

2 What does Rachel **dislike** about the countryside?

3 Name two other advantages and two disadvantages, other than those mentioned by Rachel, of living in the countryside.

What is it like to live in a city?

I live in a city. It's quite large, with about 300 000 inhabitants. There are lots of businesses, firms, shops and leisure activities. There are lots of parks and museums

I like living in a city because we're really near all the amenities and leisure activities. We can meet lots of people

My school is on the outskirts of the city. It takes about 20 minutes to get there by coach

I might like to live in the country when I'm older and retired – it would be peaceful and relaxing

I like to walk in to town and go swimming, ice-skating or to the cinema. There are lots of parks where I can meet my friends

My grandparents live in the country. I like to visit them, but I would not like to live there all the time

When I'm older I'd like to live abroad, but in a city, because there is more to do and I'm used to it

ACTION!

1 What does Andrew like about living in a city?

2 What could be some of the disadvantages of living in a city?

3 Compare Andrew's lifestyle with Rachel's (on the previous page).
(a) What are the main differences? (b) Are there any similarities?

4 What do you like and dislike about living in your local area?

UNIT 3
The European Community

THE EUROPEAN COMMUNITY: WHAT IS IT?

Twelve countries of Europe are currently members of the **'European Community'**. The main purpose of joining such a group is to improve the standard of living for everyone living in the member countries. The idea is that each country makes a contribution to the community budget and in return receives goods and services that they could not provide for themselves. (The actual amount each country contributes varies according to its wealth and population.) This creates a huge market for food and manufactured goods and trade between countries is easier. It is hoped that prices of goods become the same throughout the Community. Also, a large group of countries, with a total population of around 350 million, is a major force in the world economy.

Although there are twelve members now, not all the countries joined at the same time.

1957 Italy, France, Belgium, Luxembourg, Netherlands, West Germany
1973 United Kingdom, Eire, Denmark
1981 Greece
1984 Spain and Portugal

In future other countries – perhaps those from Eastern Europe – may express an interest in joining the Community.

The countries of the European Community

ACTION!

> Find a map of Europe in an atlas. Look at the map on the next page.
>
> **1** Name the countries numbered 1–5.
>
> **2** Name the cities lettered B, C, D, L, P.
>
> **3** What is the capital of Greece? Spain? Belgium?
>
> **4** How many countries are in the European Community?

A CLOSER LOOK AT TWO COUNTRIES OF THE EC

1 Italy

Italy was one of the original six countries which signed the 'Treaty of Rome' in 1957, setting up the beginnings of the European Community.

Italy has a population of around 58 million (almost the same as the UK) and a total area of 301 000 sq km (slightly larger than the UK).

It is a popular country for tourists to visit. The lovely beaches and Mediterranean climate attract sunseekers. It is a country that is rich in history, culture and art.

Italian food and wine is famous throughout the world and so too is its passion for sport – especially football.

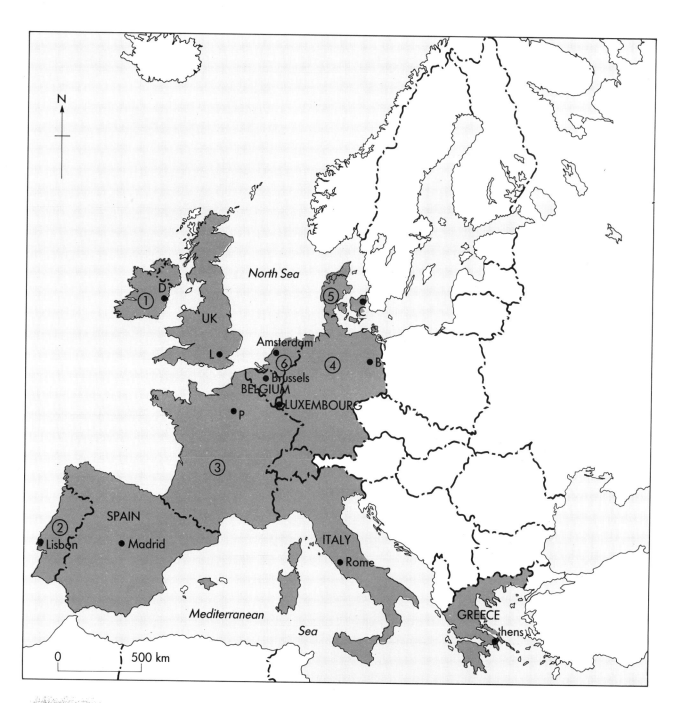

ACTION!

Find a map of Italy in an atlas.

1 Name the sea areas marked 1, 2 and 3.

2 Name the islands marked A and B.

3 Name the cities marked C, F, P, T, V.

4 Which rivers flow through:
(a) town F (b) Rome?

5 Which mountains form 'the backbone of Italy'?

Images of Italy

Contrasts in Italy

Although Italy is quite a rich country its wealth is not spread evenly. The north of Italy is heavily industrialised and its flourishing industry makes it one of the wealthiest regions in Europe. In contrast, the south of Italy has few natural resources and its agriculture, in many cases, is primitive. It is one of the poorest regions in Europe.

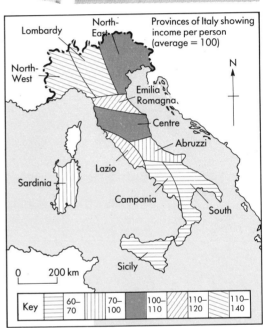

Provinces of Italy showing income per person (average = 100)

Lombardy

North-East

North-West

Emilia Romagna

Centre

Abruzzi

Lazio

Sardinia

Campania

South

Sicily

0   200 km

| Key | 60–70 | 70–100 | 100–110 | 110–120 | 110–140 |

Why is the north so rich?

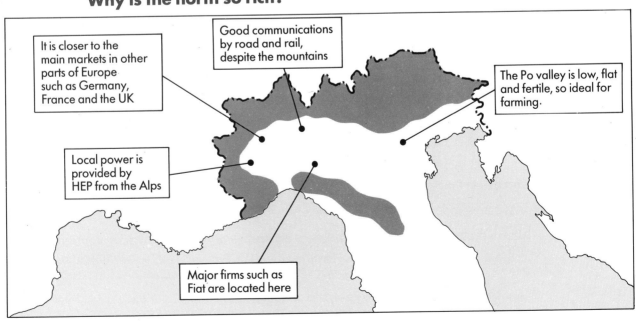

It is closer to the main markets in other parts of Europe such as Germany, France and the UK

Good communications by road and rail, despite the mountains

The Po valley is low, flat and fertile, so ideal for farming.

Local power is provided by HEP from the Alps

Major firms such as Fiat are located here

Look at the diagram on the previous page.

1 Why should 'closer to the main markets in other parts of Europe' be important for companies in northern Italy?

2 What is hydro-electric power (HEP) and why should it be important in the Alps?

Why is the south so poor?

The Mezzogiorno (the land of the Midday Sun) is the name given to the southern part of Italy. 40 per cent of Italy's population live there, but they create only 20 per cent of the country's wealth. This is mainly because:

- Much of the area is mountainous, covered with thin, infertile soil.
- Long periods of drought during the summer months make farming difficult.

- Most farms are inefficient, lacking modern machinery and irrigation.
- Many farmers don't own the land they work on.
- Yields are low. Products such as grapes, olives, fruit and wheat can be produced more cheaply in the north.
- Traditional industries are few, inefficient and use out-of-date methods.

All these problems mean that poverty can be seen everywhere with poor housing in towns and low social conditions. Many houses and farms lack the basic amenities – no running water or sanitation. Lack of jobs means people are forced to migrate to the north.

Since 1950 the Italian government and the European Community have been trying to bridge the wealth gap between the Mezzogiorno and the rest of Europe. The map opposite shows a number of ways in which they have been trying to do this.

The Taranto steelworks, Italy

Economic help for southern Italy

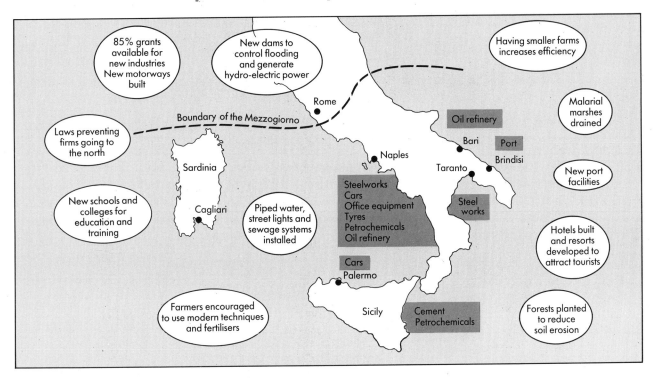

85% grants available for new industries
New motorways built

New dams to control flooding and generate hydro-electric power

Having smaller farms increases efficiency

Rome

Boundary of the Mezzogiorno

Laws preventing firms going to the north

Oil refinery

Bari

Port

Malarial marshes drained

Naples

Brindisi

Sardinia

Taranto

New port facilities

New schools and colleges for education and training

Cagliari

Piped water, street lights and sewage systems installed

Steelworks
Cars
Office equipment
Tyres
Petrochemicals
Oil refinery

Steel works

Hotels built and resorts developed to attract tourists

Cars

Palermo

Farmers encouraged to use modern techniques and fertilisers

Sicily

Cement
Petrochemicals

Forests planted to reduce soil erosion

ACTION!

From the list above, put each statement into the categories outlined below:

Designed to help social conditions

Designed to help industry

Designed to help agriculture

33

2 France

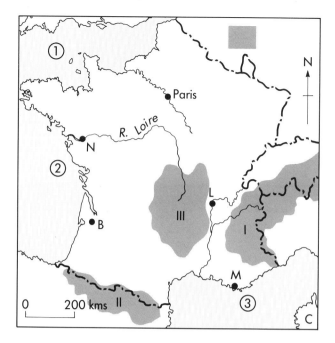

France is the largest country in the European Community – it is almost twice the size of the UK. It has a total population of about 56.3 million – slightly less than the UK.

France has been an important country throughout history and, just like Italy, France was one of the original six countries that signed the Treaty of Rome in 1957.

France, being a large country, has a tremendous variety of landscape. The north coast is very different from the south coast. Brittany in the north-west is very different from Alpine France, in the south-east. There is also a great variety of peoples, cultures and traditions. People of the French countryside are very different from the modern, fashion-conscious people of Paris.

ACTION!

Find a map of France in an atlas and look at the map above.

1 Name the sea areas marked 1, 2 and 3.

2 Name the island marked C.

3 Name the cities marked B, L, M and N.

4 Name the rivers that flow through: (a) Paris; (b) city L.

5 Name the highland areas marked I, II and III.

Contrasts in France

BRITTANY

Brittany is a part of France which has a history and culture all its own. The area was originally settled by Celts – the same people who settled in Ireland, Scotland and Wales. They even have their own language – Breton. The houses and buildings are very different in style from other parts of France.

PARIS

Paris is one of the world's leading cities. It is a wealthy city, famous for its shops and its fashion. Tourists are attracted to its many historical and cultural sites. Paris has a reputation for being Europe's most romantic city.

THE MASSIF CENTRAL

This is one of the poorer areas of France. It is a mountainous region where many people work on farms. Farming is difficult due to the steep slopes and poor soils, and because of this many people have left farming and have moved to other parts of France.

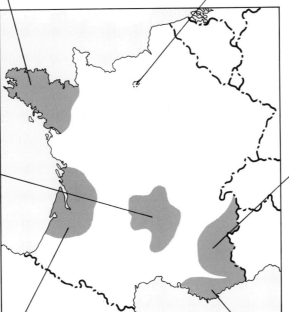

THE FRENCH ALPS

For many years the Alps had few visitors. It was a poor region and the few people who lived there earned their living through dairying. Nowadays the Alps have become a major centre for tourism. During the winter, skiers flock there in their thousands and during the summer people are attracted to the mountains for the scenery and fresh mountain air.

THE SOUTH-WEST

This part of France is flat and has an ideal climate for growing grapes. It is one of France's most important wine-producing regions. Bordeaux wines are famous throughout the world, and so too is cognac, which is also produced in this region.

THE FRENCH RIVIERA

This area is one of the 'playgrounds of the rich'. The warm summer climate and the beaches of the Mediterranean attract some of the wealthiest people in the world. It is commonplace to see large, expensive boats moored in the many marinas along the coast.

1 Which of the regions of France shown on the previous page is likely to be:
(a) The wealthiest:
(b) The poorest?
Say why in each case.

2 More foreign visitors go to France than to any other country in Europe. List the attractions each of the six regions outlined above would have for the tourist.

Paris: a closer look

Paris was originally situated on an island in the middle of the river Seine – an important defensive site. Over the centuries the city has grown steadily and is now home to over nine million people. Paris has become so important to France that it now dominates many aspects of French life.

Main area for French industry, especially cars, chemicals and electrical goods

The centre of the French government

With a population of nearly 9½ million it is 8 times larger than any other French city

Most large companies have their head-quarters in Paris

The main commercial and financial centre of France

It is a main centre for the arts and entertainment, including the main TV stations

All railways and motorways lead to Paris

With 12 universities it has 35% of all French students

Traffic congestion in Paris

The problem

- Paris has over one million cars with only 720 000 parking spaces.
- Thousands of buses and lorries use Paris streets every day.

- Paris streets are old and narrow, so traffic easily becomes congested.
- Fumes and noise lead to high levels of pollution.

Possible solutions

- Build more motorways around the edge of the city.
- Employ more tow trucks to remove illegally parked cars.
- Issue drivers with special parking permits.
- Restrict the number of cars on the road by using a number plate system – odd numbers one day, even numbers the next.

ACTION!

1 Why was it important for Paris to be built, originally, on an island?

2 (a) List three ways in which Paris dominates French life.
(b) What problems do you think this may cause the rest of France?

3 Look at each of the possible solutions to traffic problems, above. Each one could create more problems than it solves. List the problems each solution would cause.

The Massif Central: a closer look

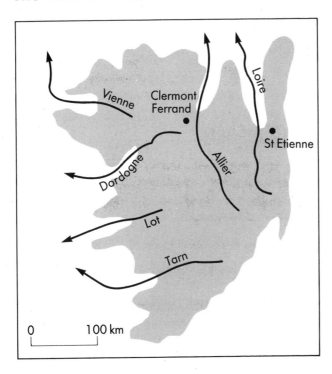

The Massif Central is a mountain region found in south central France. It is a farming region with some good land, but most of it is poor with thin soils, steep slopes and high mountains. Most farms are small, isolated and family run, where sheep and cattle are kept in small numbers. The largest town in the region is Clermont Ferrand. It is a major centre for industry – the Michelin Tyre Factory employs nearly 18 000 people. The town attracts many young people from the surrounding countryside looking for work. St. Etienne is also an industrial centre, although its importance is declining.

The problems

- High, rugged and isolated in many places. Heavy snow during winter.
- Farming is primitive and costly and products are not as cheap as those produced on efficient lowland farms.

- No facilities for young people, such as discos and cinemas.
- Farming is difficult, so farmers work hard for little profit.
- No jobs for young people, so they are forced to move out to places like Clermont Ferrand or even Paris.
- Many farms and villages are becoming abandoned.

Possible government solutions

- Farms joined together to make larger, more economical, more efficient units.
- More jobs provided for the young in forestry, craft and tourist industries.
- Better houses built to encourage young people to stay.
- Services improved with better roads and rail links.
- Abandoned farms turned into holiday cottages and second homes.
- The area has been designated a National Park and tourism encouraged.

ACTION!

1 Why is farming not as profitable on farms in the Massif Central as on lowland farms?

2 Why do you think there are so few towns in the Massif Central?

3 (a) List the reasons why young people are forced to move out.
   (b) What are the attractions of places like Clermont Ferrand for young people?

4 Why would the government want to encourage people to stay in the area?

5 Renovating old barns and farm buildings is not an ideal solution for the economy of the area. Why is this so?

TOURISM IN THE EUROPEAN COMMUNITY

Tourism is the industry that caters for people who want a holiday. Nearly 60% of people living in the European Community took a holiday of some kind during 1991. Tourism is, therefore, a major industry. It provides jobs for about 18 million people across Europe. Places people visit for a holiday are called resorts.

The tourism industry has grown rapidly over the last 30 years. This is because:

- People have more leisure time from working shorter hours, having paid leave from their work or simply retiring at a younger age;
- People have become richer, so they have more money to spend on luxuries such as holidays;
- More information is available about other places so people want to visit them;
- It is easier to get to places that were once considered far away;
- A full range of purpose-built resorts and package holidays has become available.

There are different types of holiday, and therefore each tourist area can offer a different range of facilities and activities and so attract a different type of tourist:

- Long-stay summer resorts attract people who want to spend a week or more in one centre. These resorts are usually found on the coast where there are sandy beaches and, often, warm dry summers;
- Short-stay attractions are usually visited by people on day trips or short breaks. These places have to be easy to reach;
- Cultural and historical centres tend to be in towns and cities where the visitors are people who are interested in architecture, art and history;
- Winter sports and mountains. Skiing has become very popular in the last twenty years. Mountain walking and scenic views also attract many visitors during the summer.

Tourist areas of Europe

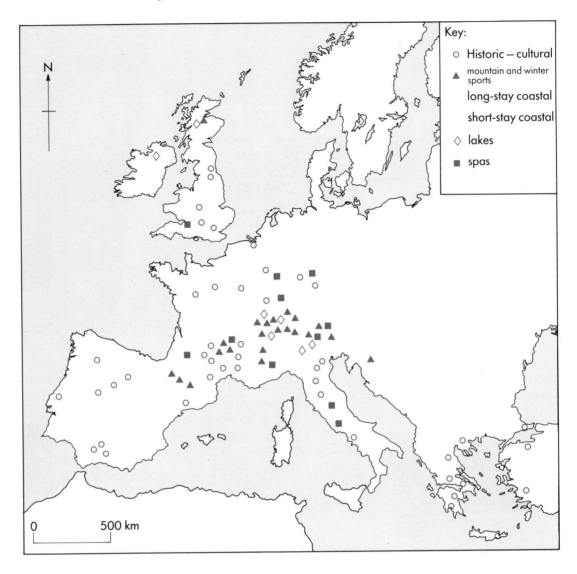

Key:
- ○ Historic – cultural
- ▲ mountain and winter sports
- long-stay coastal
- short-stay coastal
- ◇ lakes
- ■ spas

0   500 km

ACTION!

1 List six jobs associated with tourism. Think about how people book holidays, the places where they stay and how they travel there.

2 What sort of facilities would a resort require for *you* to have an enjoyable holiday?

3 Find out where your friends went on holiday. What did they do when they got there? Was it very different from your holiday experience?

4 Look at the map of Europe, above. Name the five countries that have the most long-stay coastal resorts. Why do you think there are so many resorts in these countries?

5 Why are there so few long-stay resorts in northern Europe?

Holidays in Britain

Despite the attractions of a foreign holiday, many people still take their annual holiday in this country. Britain also attracts many foreign tourists, so tourism in the UK is a very important industry. It employs nearly 6% of the population and earns almost £10 billion per year.

Scotland attracts visitors who are interested in mountain scenery and tradition. There are several winter sports resorts which open during winter months.

The Lake District and Snowdonia are very popular with people interested in hill walking and scenic views.

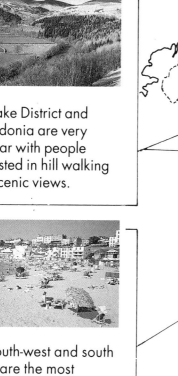

The south-west and south coast are the most popular areas in the UK for holidays. People are attracted by the fine beaches, warmer temperatures, more sunshine and more dry days.

Places such as Blackpool offer traditional British holidays with amusement arcades, funfairs, donkey rides and rock.

London attracts many thousands of foreign tourists. It is also popular with Britons looking for a short break.

Many British holidaymakers spend their time at a holiday camp. Entertainment and other indoor and outdoor activities are supplied, even when it rains. Some camps are now entirely covered with transparent 'sun roofs' and heated to a constant temperature.

N

Lake District

Blackpool

Snowdonia

London

Key:

- Most popular coastal resorts
- Most popular mountain areas
- London
- ⊙ Main holiday camps

0   200
km

ACTION!

1 Explain why many people are attracted to the south-west and south coast for their holiday.

2 Why do you think many foreign tourists spend at least some of their holiday in London?

3 What sort of people would be attracted to a holiday camp? Why?

4 Which of the holidays outlined above would be most suitable for an elderly couple? Why?

Problems associated with tourism

- During peak holiday times, roads to resorts can become crowded and congested, making journeys a nightmare.
- Small villages and holiday towns can get crowded during the summer but are extremely quiet out of season. This can make it difficult for hotels, restaurants and shops to stay in business.
- Lack of business during winter months means unemployment for many workers in tourism.

Many resorts are trying to minimise the problems by:

- Trying to extend the season by keeping places of interest open longer and encouraging people to take short breaks;
- Trying to attract business conferences to the town;
- Opening all-season attractions such as model villages, leisure centres and theatres.

Holidays in the sun

Many British people now take their holidays abroad. Holidays organised by travel agents and tour operators can be as cheap as holidays in Britain. Countries around the Mediterranean Sea have become very popular – hot, dry weather throughout the summer is virtually guaranteed and with sandy beaches and a clear, warm sea to swim in this area of Europe is very appealing. It is also easy to get to – flights to Mediterranean resorts take 2–4 hours, the same time it may take to get to a British resort.

Case study: The Greek island of Kos

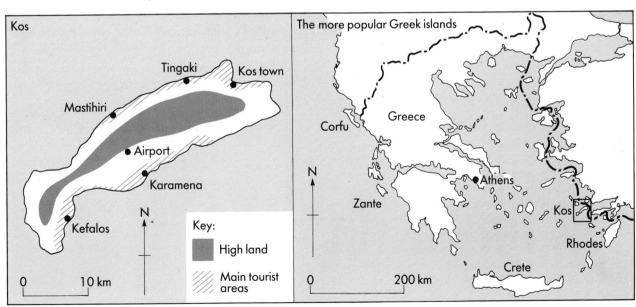

Climates compared

		April	May	June	July	Aug	Sep	Oct
Kos:	Average temperature °C	20	23	26	30	29	27	24
	Sunshine hours	8	10	12	13	12	10	8
London:	Average temperature °C	13	16	19	29	29	18	14
	Sunshine hours	5	6	7	6	6	5	4

Kos is one of the lesser known Greek Islands, although over the past ten years it has become increasingly popular with British tourists. It takes about 3 hours 50 minutes to fly there from Britain and the island offers a wide range of accommodation. It has the reputation of being very green and quiet. Its sandy beaches and a calm, warm, shallow sea make it an ideal location for families with young children. There are plenty of bars and tavernas (inns) where visitors can enjoy good food and traditional Greek dancing.

How has tourism changed the island?

Tourists are not the only people on Kos. The island has a rich history and there have been people living and working there for centuries. Tourism has brought a total change to the island – tourists want to stay in good accommodation with electricity and running water, so drainage and sanitation have been improved. There has been a change in traditional occupations, too. Sadly, more people also means more noise, litter, pollution and crime.

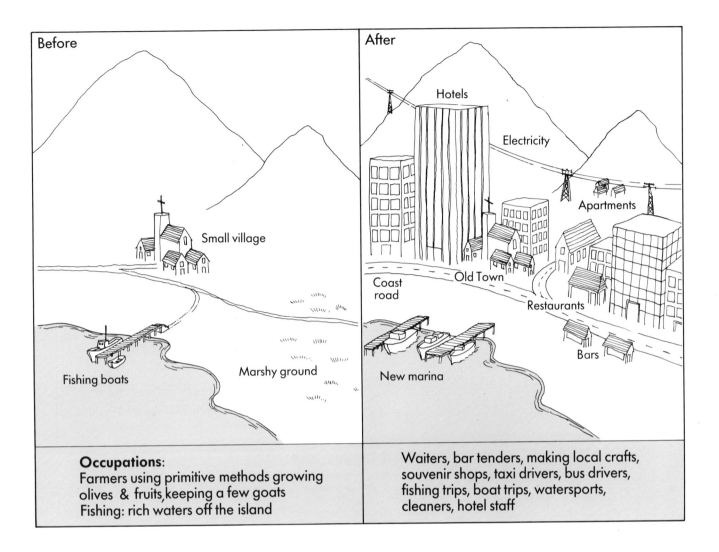

Before

After

Small village

Fishing boats

Marshy ground

Hotels

Electricity

Apartments

Coast road

Old Town

Restaurants

Bars

New marina

Occupations:
Farmers using primitive methods growing olives & fruits, keeping a few goats
Fishing: rich waters off the island

Waiters, bar tenders, making local crafts, souvenir shops, taxi drivers, bus drivers, fishing trips, boat trips, watersports, cleaners, hotel staff

ACTION!

1 Use an atlas to locate Kos. In which sea(s) is it found?

2 What are the attractions of Kos for the British tourist?

3 Use the climate figures to draw a bar graph showing the average temperature and average sunshine hours for Kos and London.

4 Look at the drawings showing Kos before and after the island became a tourist centre and list five ways in which tourism has changed the island.

Winter resorts

Since the late 1970s, winter sports holidays have been very popular, in areas such as The Alps. This had led to a huge growth in the skiing industry and in the number of tour operators offering skiing holidays. A number of purpose-built resorts have sprung up throughout The Alps to ease the pressure on the more traditional resorts. Skiing is a very specialised activity and requires specialised facilities. Ski runs (pistes) have to be prepared, ski lifts installed, hotels built, medical facilities made available and other winter facilities provided, e.g. cross-country skiing, tobogganing and ice skating. These activities take place during the winter, when it gets dark early, so the resorts usually provide a range of après-ski (evening) activities.

Case study: Val Thorens, French Alps

SKI FACTS

High altitude and glacier skiing
Snow cannons: 115
Artificial piste: 11.5km
No. of lifts: 200
Km of piste: 600km
Direction of slopes: SE, E, N, W
Mountain restaurants: 9
Easy runs: 101, Medium runs 155
   Difficult runs: 28

Après-ski: At least 20 bars and restaurants; fashion and food shops; tennis and squash; cinema; 3 discos

ACTION!

Use all the information given on this page to answer these questions:

1 Why has there been a need to build more winter sports resorts in The Alps?

2 What is meant by the terms:
(a) specialised activity;
(b) piste;
(c) après-ski?

3 Val Thorens is a 'snow sure' resort.
(a) What do you think this means?
(b) Why is it important?

4 How do you think ski resorts change the natural environment?

UNIT 4
The wider world

PHYSICAL FEATURES OF THE WORLD

ACTION!

Atlas skills 1: Physical features of the world

You will need a blank map of the world, similar to the one shown below, and an atlas.

1 Find a physical map of the world in your atlas. On your blank map mark on the following features:

(a) **Sea areas:** Pacific Ocean, Indian Ocean, North Atlantic Ocean, South Atlantic Ocean, Southern Ocean, Arctic Ocean, Caribbean Sea.

(b) **Mountain ranges:** Rockies, Andes, Himalayas.

(c) **Rivers:** Colorado, Mississippi, St. Lawrence, Amazon, Congo or Zaire, Nile, Zambesi, Volga, Ganges, Yangtze, Murray/Darling.

(d) **Other features:** The Great Lakes in North America, the Sahara Desert in North Africa.

2 (a) Join up each of the latitude lines marked. Label each line correctly with one of the following: Equator, Tropic of Capricorn, Tropic of Cancer, Arctic Circle, Antarctic Circle.

(b) Mark on the prime meridian and the International Date Line.

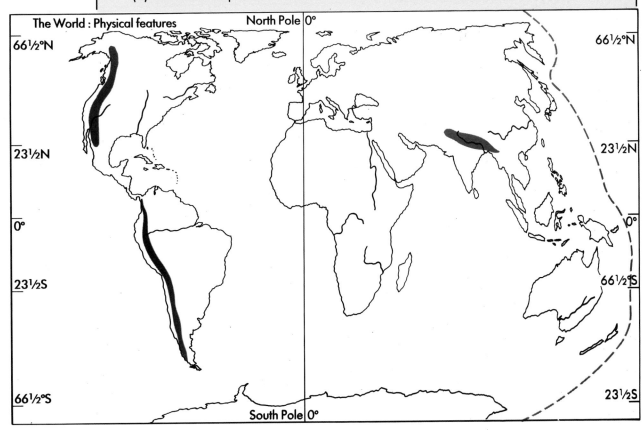

The World : Physical features

3 Shade all the land area in light green.

4 (a) Name two rivers which are found in the Southern Hemisphere.

(b) Name one mountain range that runs across the Equator.

5 What is the International Date Line?

ACTION!

Atlas skills 2: Continents, countries and cities

For this exercise you need a blank copy of a world map (see below) and an atlas.

1 On your blank map of the world label the following continents:
Africa; Europe; Asia; North America; South America; Antarctica; Australasia.

2 Use your atlas to locate the following countries, then shade them lightly on your blank map and correctly label them:
USSR; Japan; Australia; New Zealand; South Africa; USA; Canada; Mexico; Brazil; Argentina; Egypt; Peru; Ghana; Venezuela; Saudi Arabia; Indonesia; India; Israel; Bangladesh; China; Nigeria; Italy; Germany; Kenya; Pakistan.

3 Each of the black dots on the map is one of the world's major cities. Use your atlas to label correctly these cities listed below:
Beijing; Sydney; Johannesburg; Jakarta; Sao Paulo; Moscow; Jerusalem; Delhi; Tokyo; New York; Singapore; Los Angeles; Toronto; Mexico City; Cairo; Washington DC; Accra; Bombay; St Petersburg (formerly Leningrad); Calcutta; Shanghai; Lagos; Nairobi; Buenos Aires; San Francisco; Lima; Chicago.

4 Each of the stars on the map has a number. Join the stars using a black pen. Write above the completed line 'Developed North' and below the line write 'Developing South'.

5 Locate the Panama and Suez Canals and add them to your map.

ECONOMIC DEVELOPMENT ACROSS THE WORLD

Some countries are much richer than others. We can work out how rich or how poor a country is by looking at how much the people earn, how many things they own, how much they eat, how many of the children go to school and how healthy the population is.

Wealthy countries are rich because they have **developed** their resources. They have spent their money on building good schools, good roads and investing in health care. Poor countries are poor because they are still **developing** their resources. They find it very difficult to get enough money to build good schools, build good roads and develop an efficient health service.

Three countries compared

	Italy	Brazil	Bangladesh
Status	Rich	Middle Income	Poor
GNP per head (£)	7016	1354	104
Life expectancy	73 yrs	65 yrs	51 yrs
Infant mortality	10/1000	63/1000	135/1000
People/doctor ratio	349	2402	10 925
Literacy rates	93%	76%	29%

GNP per head: Gross national product is the total value of everything produced in that country. When divided by the number of people living in that country it gives an indication of how wealthy people are.

Life expectancy: How long people in that country are expected to live.

Infant mortality: The number of babies who die before their first birthday.

People/doctor ratio: The total number of people divided by the number of doctors. It gives an indication of how quickly you would be able to see a doctor if you were ill.

Literacy rates: The percentage of the population who can read and write.

ACTION!

1 Find a map of the world in an atlas and locate the three countries listed above.

2 You will need to look at all the information in the table to answer the following questions:

(a) In which country do people live longest? Suggest three reasons why this might be so.

(b) Suggest two reasons why infant mortality rates are so high in Bangladesh.

(c) People being able to read and write is very important if a country wishes to improve the overall standard of living. Why do you think this is so?

All countries are not the same!

Economic activity can be divided into:

Primary Activity: Concerned with extracting or using the Earth's natural resources, e.g. forestry, mining, farming and fishing.

Secondary Activity: Concerned with making things in factories (**manufacturing**) or putting parts together in **assembly plants** to form finished products, e.g. cars.

Tertiary Activity: Concerned with offering a service, e.g. a bank, a teacher, or transport.

The percentage of the workforce employed in each sector gives a good indication of how developed a country is. For example:

Italy

Much of Italian agriculture is modernised using fertilisers and machinery. People do not have to grow their own food – they can afford to buy it. They are then free to do other jobs.

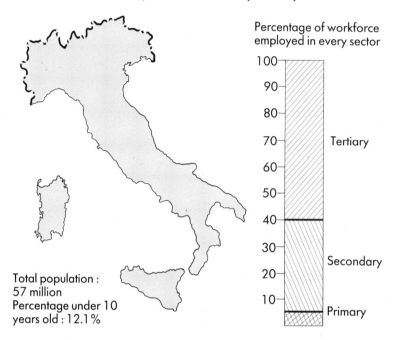

Total population : 57 million
Percentage under 10 years old : 12.1%

Percentage of workforce employed in every sector

Tertiary
Secondary
Primary

Brazil

Brazil borrowed a lot of money in the 1970s from the World Bank to build factories. Many people moved from the countryside to the towns in order to look for jobs.

Many people are still employed in the primary sector as Brazil has yet to develop fully its vast resources found in rainforest areas.

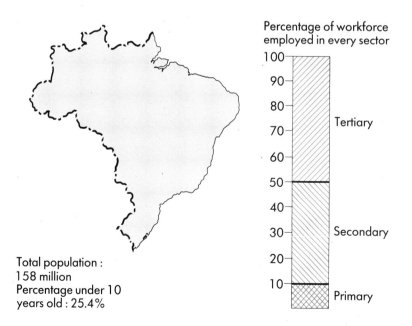

Total population : 158 million
Percentage under 10 years old : 25.4%

Percentage of workforce employed in every sector

Tertiary
Secondary
Primary

Bangladesh

Many Bangladeshis have no income with which to buy food. So most use primitive farming methods to grow their own. There are few factories in Bangladesh.

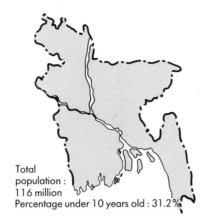

Total population : 116 million
Percentage under 10 years old : 31.2%

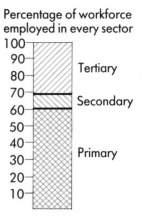

Percentage of workforce employed in every sector

- Tertiary
- Secondary
- Primary

ACTION!

In the table below place each of the following statements under the correct heading.

Many employed in agriculture
Few employed in agriculture
Factories need a lot of workers
Factories use machines and robots to do many of the jobs
Many people employed in the tertiary sector
Fewer people employed in the tertiary sector

Farming is very primitive, using the simplest of tools
Farming is advanced, using modern machines and fertilisers
Factory workers work long hours for low wages
Factory workers work for a set time and set wage each week

A developed country	A developing country

British employment structure

The employment structure not only varies between countries but can also vary within the same country from time to time. During the mid-nineteenth century Britain was beginning to industrialise and starting to develop its own resources. The employment structure then was very different to what it is today.

	1861	**1961**
Primary	32%	2%
Secondary	47%	38%
Tertiary	21%	60%

ACTION!

1 Construct a divided bar graph for Britain, for each year based on the figures outlined above.

2 Suggest two reasons why there has been such a change in the employment structure over the past 130 years.

AN IN-DEPTH STUDY: BANGLADESH

Bangladesh is a very flat, low-lying country formed at the mouth of the great rivers Ganges, Brahmaputra and Meghna.

Bangladesh is one of the poorest countries in the world, with most people living well below the poverty line.

Most Bangladeshis live in the countryside – only 16 per cent live in towns.

The land is very fertile. Annual flooding spreads rich river mud over the plains.

Most people are farmers. They have to grow their own rice to feed their families.

The climate is hot all year round, with a wet season between June and September.

Bangladesh has a population density of about 390 per sq km.

Information table

Total population	116 million
Area	144 000 sq km
Rate of population growth	2.6 per cent per year
Percentage of population in urban areas	15.7
Percentage of workers in: Farming, forestry, fishing, mining	61
Manufacturing	8
Services	31
Life expectancy	51 years
Percentage of population under 15 years	45
Average income per person	US $130 per year
Percentage of population able to read and write	29
Population ratio per doctor	10 925

ACTION!

1 Find a map of south-east Asia in an atlas.
   (a) Name the countries surrounding Bangladesh marked 1–5 on the map.
   (b) Name the sea area marked A.
   (c) Name the line of latitude marked with a broken line.

2 Look at the information table above. Bangladesh has a high proportion of its population aged under 15. What problems do you think this could bring?

3 Give two reasons why most Bangladeshis are farmers.

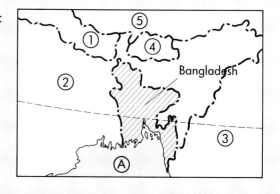

WHAT IS IT LIKE TO LIVE IN BANGLADESH?

Most people in Bangladesh live in rural areas, making their living working on the land and living in small village communities.

Houses are huts made out of whatever building materials are available – clay, branches or corrugated tin, for example.

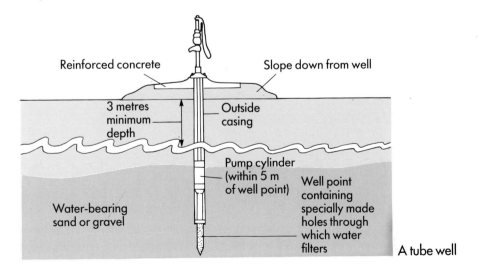

Reinforced concrete · Slope down from well

3 metres minimum depth · Outside casing

Pump cylinder (within 5 m of well point)

Well point containing specially made holes through which water filters

Water-bearing sand or gravel

A tube well

Life in the villages is very basic. There are no sanitation facilities and water is usually obtained from a village pump or well or from the local river or stream. There is no electricity.

There are few schools. The children lucky enough to have a place in a school often face a long walk each day to get there.

ACTION!

1 Choose any two of the scenes outlined in the photographs above and in each case describe what is happening.

2 Imagine we had photographs of similar activities, but this time taken in Britain. What differences would you expect to see?

A DAY IN THE LIFE OF A BANGLADESHI FAMILY

Family: Father aged 34

Mother aged 30

Children aged 14, 12, 10, 8, 6

Morning: Mother gets up, washes, dresses and prepares breakfast for her husband and children from curry leftover from the night before. After breakfast father goes with the two eldest children to their fields which have to be prepared before planting the next rice crop.

Mother keeps the youngest child with her and sends the other two to the village well to fetch some water. (The nearest school is four kilometers away but there are no places for the children so they help their parents.)

When the children return they have to go to the village laundry – a stream which runs past the village – to do the washing.

Lunchtime: Mother prepares a meal of chappatis and vegetables. One of the children takes some food out to the fields for the others.

Afternoon: Mother leaves the youngest child with an elderly neighbour and takes the other two children to gather firewood. They have to walk several kilometres carrying heavy bundles of sticks.

Evening: Father and two eldest children return from the fields. The oxen are fed and watered. Mother prepares the evening meal of rice and some curry. After the meal is cleared away it has begun to get dark. The family cannot afford oil lamps, so it is time for bed.

ACTION!

1 Read the information about a day in the life of a Bangladeshi family. List all the jobs done by:
(a) The father   (b) The mother   (c) The children

2 Where is the village laundry?

3 Which phrase suggests that the farming methods are primitive?

4 What do the family use for fuel?

HAZARDS BANGLADESH COULD DO WITHOUT

Bangladesh is a country that has always suffered from flooding. The country itself owes its existence to the rivers depositing huge amounts of silt. This silt gradually builds up, forming a flat plan just above sea level. Much of Bangladesh is less than 15m above sea level.

The 1991 floods in Bangladesh

Many millions of people live in these low-lying lands as the regular flooding and fertile soils form ideal conditions for rice to grow.

Flooding can come from the rivers or the sea. During springtime, snow melting in the mountains can cause river levels to rise and the risk of flooding to increase.

By far the most destructive and life-threatening floods come from the sea. Violent storms called typhoons form out over the Indian Ocean (usually during the autumn).

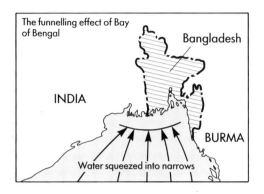
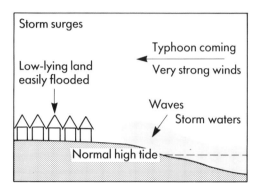

Occasionally these storms head straight towards Bangladesh. Sea water is driven northwards by the strong winds and funnels into the Bay of Bengal. The extra amount of water and huge waves can easily wash over the low-lying land. Many people may die, as they do not have radios or televisions to warn them that a storm is coming.

ACTION!

Read all the information above.

1 Why is regular flooding by rivers beneficial to Bangladesh?

2 What is a typhoon?

3 Explain why the shape of the Bay of Bengal increases the effects of typhoons.

4 Every time a typhoon hits Bangladesh thousands die. Give three reasons why the loss of life is always so great.

AN IN-DEPTH STUDY: BRAZIL

Facts, figures and distribution of population

Information table

Total population	158 million	Percentage of population under 15 years	36.3
Area	8 511 965 sq km	Average income per person	US $2051 per year
Rate of population growth	2.37 per cent per year	Percentage of population able to read and write	76
Percentage of population in urban areas	70.8	Population ratio per doctor	2402
Percentage of workers in:			
Farming, forestry, fishing, mining	11		
Manufacturing	39		
Services	50		
Life expectancy	Male 62 years; Female 67 years		

The river Amazon is surrounded by the largest rainforest in the world.

Brazil is the largest country in South America and the fifth largest in the world in area.

The north-east region is a semi-desert.

Brazil is trying to develop its resources by 'opening up' the interior.

Brazil is the sixth largest country in the world in terms of population.

The north and centre have few people living there due to their being remote and inaccessible.

Most people in Brazil live in the east and south-east of the country.

Most people in Brazil are very poor.

Manaus

Belem

North

North East

Recife

Salvador

Centre West

South East

Brasilia

Belo Horizonte

Rio de Janeiro

South

Sao Paulo

Key:

	0–9%
	10–19%
	20–29%
	30–39%
	40–49%

0   800 km

ACTION!

Find a map of South America in an atlas to help you answer these questions, and fill in the map shown above.

1 (a) Name the countries surrounding Brazil marked 1 – 10 on the map.

   (b) Name the sea areas marked A and B.

   (c) Name the two lines of latitude marked C and D.

2 Look at all the information on the previous page. Brazil has a high proportion of its population aged under 15. What problems do you think this could bring?

3 Why are there very few people living in the north of Brazil?

Ecuador

Brazil

55

Life in Brazil 1: A country of contrasts

Differences in wealth exist not only between countries of the world, but are also found within countries. Some parts of Brazil are very wealthy, with all the attractions of a modern society. Other parts, however, are extremely poor, with many people living in the worst poverty imaginable. Two such contrasting areas are south-east Brazil, with over two thirds of the country's income, and the north-east, which is very poor.

South-east Brazil

Copacabana beach in Rio

Carnival time in Rio

Reasons for wealth:

- Most of Brazil's industry is concentrated here.
- Coffee is an important Brazilian export and many wealthy coffee plantations are found in this region.
- It has the natural energy resource of HEP.
- Roads and railways in this area are well-developed.

North-east Brazil

Problems:

- Low incomes.
- High unemployment.
- Very poor living conditions in villages and towns.

Living on the edge of Rio

Reasons for poverty:

- A lack of rich farm resources and valuable minerals.
- Occasional droughts affect crop production.
- A small number of wealthy families and companies own the land.
- There is a lack of investment in the area by the government and foreign companies.

This table shows the contrasts in population and wealth between different regions in Brazil:

Region	Population (% of total)	Share of income (% of total)
North	4	2
Centre West	6	3.1
South	18.1	18.3
South-East	42.2	62.8
North-East	29.7	13.8

ACTION!

Look carefully at the photograph of the young man from south-east Brazil and the two photographs of poverty in north-east Brazil.

The people in the photographs were asked their opinions of life in Brazil. The two paragraphs below are their answers.

1 Using the words in the box, complete the two paragraphs.

'This is a _____ climate to live in, the sun always shines. My father is a wealthy _____. He made his money from the profits of his _____ plantation. I have an important job within our company. I am responsible for _____. I spend lots of time going to _____ and eating out – life can be so hectic sometimes. It's great when the Mardi Gras comes around, I get _____ for a whole week. I love being Brazilian.'

'Life is okay sometimes but most of the time it is one big _____ . My father does _____ to provide me and my six brothers with enough food. We live in a comfortable _____ although it does get a little dirty and _____ sometimes. My job is to fetch the clean _____ everyday. I hope one day to be able to move to the big city and have a _____ job. I think I could be very good at washing cars.'

shack	parties	proper	superb	his best	struggle	coffee	exports
overcrowded	water	drunk	businessman				

2 Which paragraph describes life in north-east Brazil and which one describes south-east Brazil?

3 From these paragraphs what can you tell about the lifestyle of the people involved?

4 How do the two paragraphs together reflect modern Brazil?

Life in Brazil 2: The rainforest

Much of northern Brazil has very few people living in it because it is part of the huge Amazon rainforest. It is a source of great wealth, for many different reasons:

- The trees provide valuable timber, much in demand for furniture making.
- The leaves, bark and roots of many of the forest plants provide us with important medicines.
- The rainforest itself is home to many different species of plants, animals, birds and insects.
- The vast numbers of trees produce much of the oxygen in the air.

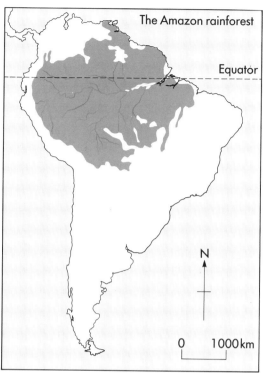

The Amazon rainforest

Equator

N

0   1000km

Who lives in the rainforest?

The native inhabitants of the Amazon rainforest are tribal Indians. It is not known for certain when the Indians first settled in the forests, nor where they came from, but it is thought that they have been living their traditional way of life for thousands of years. This way of life was very simple — the forest provided all their building materials, medicines and weapons. Their food came from a variety of sources. They: **hunted** for meat and skins; **gathered** fruits, berries, nuts and edible plants; **fished** in the many rivers; **farmed** using simple 'slash and burn' agriculture.

'Slash and burn' involved cutting down and burning a small area of forest, the ashes being used as a fertiliser. (Rainforest soils are very poor and useless for full-scale crop growing.) After a couple of years the soil would lose its nourishment, so the tribe of Indians would move on to another patch of forest. The abandoned clearing was soon overgrown by the forest again. Hunting in a different area would also allow the old area to recover its population of animals. Using the forest in this way did no permanent damage.

1 Look at the drawing above, which shows a typical Amazonian Indian scene. Match each of the following statements with their correct number:

(a) hunting in the forest; (b) fishing nets hanging out to dry; (c) a dug out canoe; (d) wood cut for fuel; (e) communal hut for sleeping; (f) crops growing in the 'garden'; (g) cooking using clay pots; (h) a hammock for sleeping; (i) food already gathered.

2 Name four items shown in the diagram made of wood, and three made of grasses or reeds.

Opening up the rainforest

Brazil is a very large country, with a large population. Most of these people live in one of the cities of the south and east. The cities were becoming so overcrowded and Brazil was becoming so poor that during the mid 1960s the Brazilian government took the decision to open up the rainforest areas

The trans-Amazonian highway

Opencast mining

Their aim was to:
- develop the vast resources that lay within and beneath the Amazonian area;
- develop new industry which would create wealth for Brazil;
- create more land for settlement, where people could farm their own land and so move out of the crowded cities.

Vast areas of rainforest were cut down as new roads and towns were built; new farms were created; and areas of opencast mining were developed.

Cutting down the rainforest has created many problems:

Valuable timber is simply being burned, which increases the carbon dioxide levels of the atmosphere. This could affect the world's climate.

Many plants, animals and insect species will be wiped out and lost forever.

Soils are very poor, so growing crops is unsuccessful.

Much of the land is now given over to grazing cattle for American hamburgers.

Indian tribes are losing their land, their culture and their hunting grounds. Their traditional way of life is being lost forever. They are being forced into cities, where they live in desperate poverty.

Much of the soil is washed into rivers, which are silting up and flooding more frequently.

Remember: once the rainforest has been destroyed it will never grow again – it is lost FOREVER.

ACTION!

Changes in the Amazon rainforest

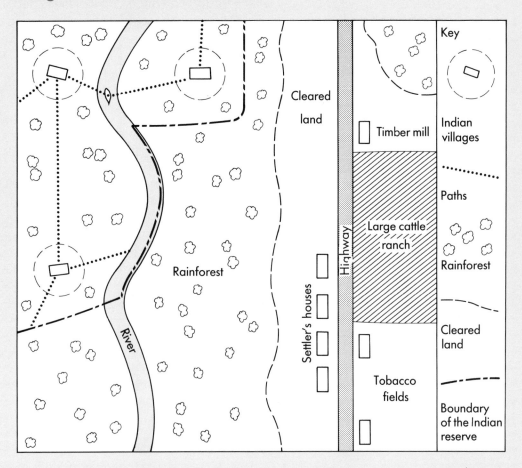

1 What was this area like before white settlers moved in?

2 Describe the main changes that have taken place.

3 How has it been possible for settlers to clear large areas of rainforest?

4 Why are the settlers' houses built near the highway?

5 How do the settlers make a living in the forest?

6 How would you feel about the changes if you were:
   • an Indian living in this area;
   • the owner of the large cattle ranch, who lives in the USA;
   • the wife of a poor white settler who works in the timber mill?

7 Do you think it is good that a reserve has been created for the Indians?

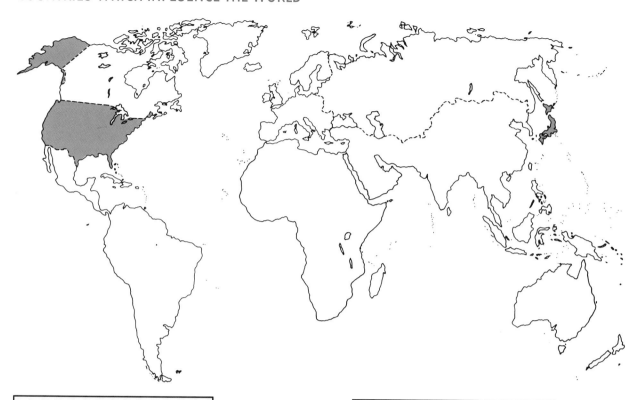

The United States of America

Area = 9 363 123 km^2
Population = 251 million
Gross national product
per capita = $19 197

Main imports:
Oil
Machinery
Vehicles
Foodstuffs
Chemicals

Main exports:
Machinery
Chemicals
Foodstuffs
Consumer goods

Japan

Area = 372 313 km^2
Population = 124 million
Gross national product
per capita = $16 289

Main imports:
Oil
Metal ores
Raw materials
Foodstuffs
Machinery

Main exports:
Machinery
Vehicles
Iron and steel
Electrical goods
Semi-conductors

AN IN-DEPTH STUDY: INDUSTRY IN JAPAN

Japan is a remarkable country.

- In 1945 it was totally devastated after World War II.
- It has very few raw materials of its own.
- It has no oil and very little of other energy resources.
- It is a mountainous country with only 14% of its land flat enough to build on.

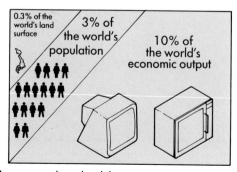

Yet despite all these problems today Japan is one of the world's leading industrial nations. In 1988 Japan:

- Produced more cars than any other country in the world.
- Made 15% of the world's steel.
- Launched more ships than anyone else.
- Made more television and radios than the whole of Europe.
- Made more watches than Switzerland.
- Produced more high quality cameras than Germany.
  Today Japan is making significant advances in computer technology and is a world force in the aircraft and space industries.

Industrial areas of Japan

Most of Japanese industry is found around the coast, close to the main cities. This is mainly because Japan is heavily dependent on imported raw materials. The shallow bays and sheltered inlets offer ideal locations for ports.

Also, many of the large factories are built on flat land reclaimed from the sea. It is easier to reclaim land when the sea is shallow.

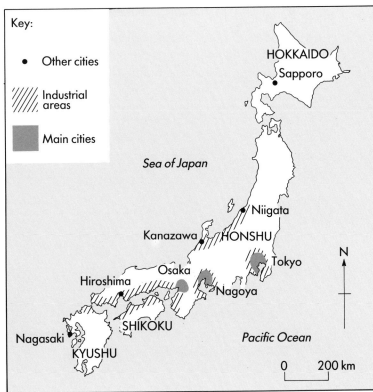

Use an atlas or the map on the previous page.

1 Complete these sentences:
(a) Japan is made up of many islands. The four main islands are _____;
(b) Japan is part of the continent of _____;
(c) the capital city of Japan is _____ .

2 List four things that can be bought in British shops that are made by Japanese companies.

H	N	I	K	K	O	N
U	I	U	P	H	A	S
Z	S	T	S	Y	D	U
S	S	O	A	Z	N	Z
H	A	Y	N	C	O	U
A	N	O	Y	Y	H	K
R	S	T	O	M	K	I
P	Y	A	M	A	H	A

3 (a) Find these Japanese companies hidden in the word square:
Suzuki, Toyota, Honda, Sharp, Sanyo, Nikkon, Yamaha, Sony, Hitachi.
(b) What sort of things does each company make?

4 Give two reasons why Japanese industry has developed along the coast.

5 Suggest two reasons why Japanese companies have become so successful.

Japan and international trade

Japan has few natural resources itself so it relies heavily on importing all its fuel and raw materials.

But the Japanese people are very skilful in turning those imported raw materials into high quality manufactured goods. Japanese workers are so good at making things that Japan has a very favourable balance of trade – that means the total value of exports is greater than the total cost of imports.

Product	In millions of dollars	
	Cost of imports	Value of exports
Food	14.4	0.7
Tea/coffee	0.7	—
Fuels and minerals	29.4	0.3
Chemicals	7.4	4.5
Manufactured goods	16.6	22.8
Machinery and transport	10.1	70.0
Total of all goods and services	126 408	209 151

Source: Geographical Digest, 1990–1

Where does it all come from?

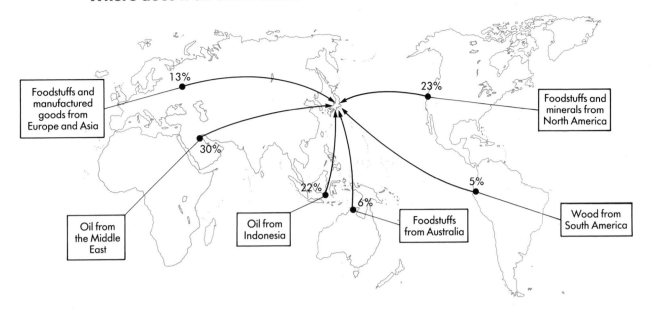

Where does it all go?

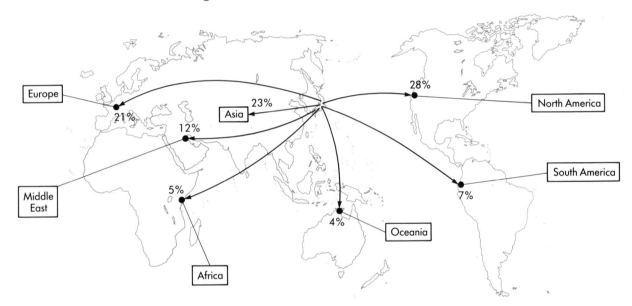

Goods exported include: cars; iron and steel; metals; radios; tape recorders; televisions; optical instruments; motor cycles; transistors; plastics; synthetic fibres; machinery; calculators.

ACTION!

1 What is meant by the following terms?
   Imports, exports, balance of trade, manufactured goods.

2 Look at the table on the previous page. Which products does Japan import more of than export?

3 (a) Look at the two maps above. Name one area of the world that Japan imports more from than it exports to.

   (b) Why do you think the percentage of imports from the area identified in (a) is so high?

4 Use the figures in the table overleaf to draw a divided bar graph. The first two sections have been drawn for you.

65

Japanese goods: percentage used for home market and exports

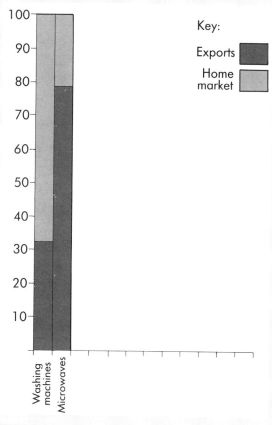

Key:

Exports ▮

Home market ▯

Goods	Percentage exported	Percentage used for home market
Washing machines	32	68
Microwaves	78	22
Pianos	29	71
Bicycles	13	87
Watches	83	17
Cameras	82	18
Calculators	76	24
Colour TVs	60	40
Refrigerators	25	75
Motor cycles	46	54
Batteries	29	71
Video recorders	82	18

5 Suggest two reasons why international trade is necessary.

UNIT 5
The active Earth

EARTHQUAKES

Every now and again we hear on the news that an earthquake has caused widespread damage and death somewhere in the world. These events are timely reminders of the destructive powers of this planet on which we live. Earthquakes are very common. Most, however, are so small that they can only be detected by sensitive scientific instruments. They only become news when major centres of population are affected.

Earthquake damage in Alaska

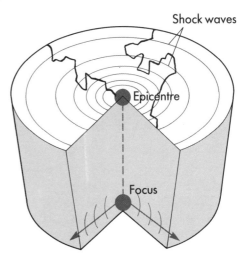

An earthquake is a series of shock waves passing through the rocks of the Earth's crust. Most last for less than a minute but in that time, the shaking ground causes many buildings to collapse, roads and railways to crack, and gas and water mains to fracture. They may even lead to huge tidal waves called **tsunamis**. It is falling masonry, flying glass and fire which kill many people during and after an earthquake.

The Richter Scale	
< 3.5	Only recorded by sensitive instruments
3.5–4.8	Feels like a lorry passing
4.9–5.4	Loose things fall
5.5–6.1	Walls crack
6.2–6.9	Chimneys fall. Some buildings collapse
7.0–7.3	Many buildings fall. Landslides
7.4–8.1	Most buildings and bridges destroyed
> 8.1	Total destruction

A seismograph

Earthquakes occur deep within the Earth where the pressure that has built up in the crust is suddenly released. The exact place where it occurs is called the **focus**. The point on the surface immediately above the focus is called the **epicentre**. The magnitude or intensity of an earthquake is measured on the Richter Scale and recorded on a seismograph.

Case study: The human response to an earthquake – Mexico City, 1985

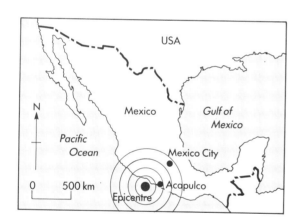

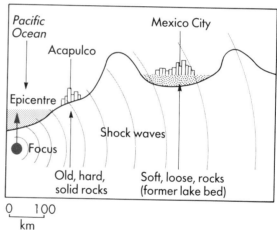

At 8.43 am on September 19th 1985, just as the morning rush hour was coming to a close, an earthquake measuring 7.8 on the Richter scale struck the 18 million inhabitants of Mexico City.

Schools, apartments, office blocks, churches and hotels came crashing down. Fires broke out as gas mains exploded. First pictures suggested that about one-third of the city had been devastated. President Miguel de la Madrid declared the city a disaster area and appealed for international help.

Rescue work went on in appalling conditions. They had to work quickly to free the thousands of business people, families and tourists trapped under the rubble. There was no light, no water and only limited amounts of petrol. Police feared that further tremors would cause more buildings to collapse. Communications were non-existent and many streets were blocked with debris. It was impossible to tell how many people had died.

Hospitals still able to operate were working on full emergency, although blood for the injured was running out and the government appealed for donors.

ACTION!

Read the passage carefully and look at the photographs and diagrams on the previous page before answering the questions.

1   Why was the timing of the earthquake important?

2   What problems were caused by the earthquake?

3   What problems did rescue workers face?

4   Why was it impossible to tell how many had died?

5   Approximately how far was Mexico City from the epicentre?

6   Acapulco was much closer to the epicentre than Mexico City, yet it suffered less damage. Look at the diagrams carefully and suggest a reason for this.

VOLCANOES

Volcanoes are another way in which the Earth displays its awesome power. Volcanic eruptions can be very explosive with vast quantities of dust, ash and gases being sent high into the atmosphere.

Volcanoes form where the molten material inside the Earth, called **magma**, is allowed to escape to the surface. When the magma reaches the surface it can be as hot as 1000°C. It cools very quickly and as it does so it builds up a cone shaped mountain. Some volcanoes, called composites, have alternate layers of ash and lava. This represents the remnants of previous eruptions.

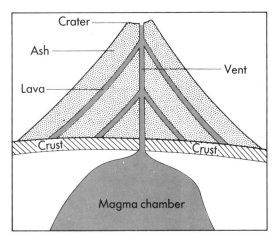

'Runny' lava

Beneath each volcano is found a large magma chamber. This is where magma and gases build up before an eruption. In the world today there are about 300 **active** volcanoes that are capable of erupting at any time. Others are **dormant**, meaning they haven't erupted for a long time but are still capable of doing so. There are also many **extinct** volcanoes, which are totally dead.

Volcanic eruptions are all different. Some volcanoes produce hot, runny lava, capable of flowing long distances. Others produce very little lava, but when they erupt they produce vast quantities of ash which can bury whole villages.

Case study: Volcanic eruption – Mount St. Helen's, 1980

Timetable of events

1978 Geologists warn that Mount St. Helen's is the most recently active cone in US mainland.

1980 *20th March.* Earthquake shakes the volcano.

27th March Ash blows out of the vent. Hazard alert is issued.

29th April. Second alert is issued as a bulge appears on the mountainside.

18th May. Mount St. Helen's blows its top, losing 400m in height.

Late May. Further eruptions of ash occur.

Mid Oct. Lava dome falls in to block the vent.

ACTION!

1 Make a sketch map of each of the photographs shown above and on page 70 showing the eruption and describe in words what has happened.

2 How has the landscape been changed by the eruption?

3 What clues did scientists have that an eruption was about to occur?

4 Mount St. Helen's is now a tourist attraction. Why do you think this is so?

The crust of the Earth

The Earth's crust is composed of a series of ridged 'plates' that fit together like pieces of a jigsaw. These plates float on the molten interior of the Earth and so move independently of each other. It is where one plate comes into contact with another that many of the world's major earthquakes and volcanoes can be found. The plate boundaries are where we find the 'active' areas of the world. The study of the movement of these plates is called **plate tectonics**.

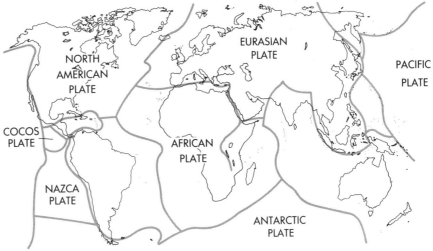

ACTION!

Major earthquakes				Major volcanoes	
Year	**Location**	**Intensity**			
1920	Southern China	8.6		Mount St. Helen's	USA
1968	Japan	8.6		Mount Shasta	USA
1964	Alaska	8.5		Aconcagua	Argentina
1962	Chile	8.5		Paricutin	Mexico
1927	S E China	8.3		Mauno Loa	Hawaii
1923	Japan	8.3		Popocatapeti	Mexico
1906	San Francisco	8.3		Surtsey	Iceland
1976	S China	8.0		Vesuvius	Italy
1985	Mexico	7.8		Etna	Italy
1987	Armenia	7.5		Cotopaxi	Ecuador
1985	Chile	7.4		Stromboli	Italy
1968	Iran	7.4		Tristan de Cunha	South Atlantic
1980	Italy	7.2		Kilimanjaro	Tanzania
1988	San Francisco	6.9		Fuji Yama	Japan
1963	Yugoslavia	6.0		Krakatoa	Indonesia

Use an atlas to:

1 (a) On a blank world map, mark the plate boundaries.
   (b) Mark each major earthquake with a blue dot.
   (c) Mark each major volcano with a red dot.

2 What do you notice about the distribution of most of the major earthquakes and volcanoes? How do you account for this?

3 Why do you think there are no major volcanoes or earthquakes in Britain at the present time?

UNIT 6
The hydrological cycle

WATER, WATER EVERYWHERE!

About two-thirds of the Earth's surface is covered by water, with nearly 97.5 per cent being salt water and only 2.5 per cent being fresh water. By far the greatest amount of water is found in the oceans. Evaporation, especially in hot climates, allows water to be transferred from the surface to the air. Winds blow moist air around until eventually it falls back to the surface as rain, snow or some other form of precipitation. Only about 21 per cent of all precipitation falls over the land and when it does, it can either:

• soak into the soil and rocks and become part of groundwater;
• remain frozen and become part of an ice sheet or glacier;
• stay on the surface as part of a river or lake;
• be taken up and used by plants;
• or be quickly evaporated back into the air.

All water will eventually end up back in the ocean. It may take a long time, as in the case of an ice sheet, or be very quick as in the case of rain falling directly into the sea. The **water cycle** means that over the whole globe the amount of water taken out of the oceans through evaporation is exactly equal to the amount washed in by rivers.

Important water words

Precipitation: water in its many forms falling from the sky as rain, hail, snow, frost and dew.

Condensation: the change from water vapour to liquid water. As air rises in the atmosphere it cools, condensation occurs and clouds form.

Evaporation: the change from liquid water to water vapour. Usually happens when the surface of the Earth is warmed.

Transpiration: water given off by plants.

Run off: water running across the surface of the land, usually as a river.

Throughflow: water running underground through the rocks.

Groundwater: water stored in the rocks as part of the water table.

	water storage times	
Atmosphere	Hours ⟶	Weeks
Surface	Days ⟶	Hundreds of years
Groundwater	One year ⟶	Thousands of years
Ice sheets	Tens of thousands of years	
Oceans	Years ⟶	Tens of thousands of years

ACTION!

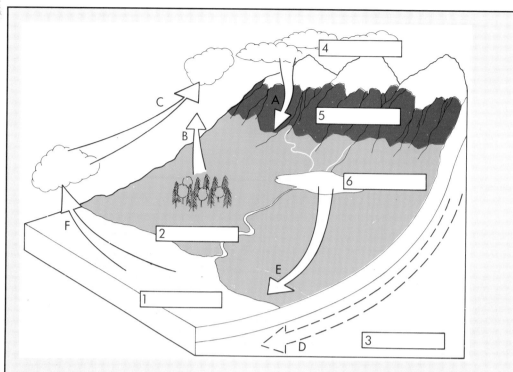

The diagram above shows the stores and links within the water cycle. Each numbered box shows a store and each lettered arrow shows a link. Match the words below with their correct letter or number.

Groundwater   snow and ice   atmosphere   plants   throughflow
run off   precipitation   ocean   transpiration   condensation   evaporation
rivers and lakes

THE RIVER STORY

Much of the water that falls from the sky as precipitation ends up in a river. All rivers begin their lives as small trickles somewhere up in the hills. The start of a river is called its **source**. As it starts to move downhill it creates for itself a narrow **channel** along which it flows. The edges of the **channel** are marked by the river's banks. Near its source the river channel is narrow but as it moves downstream, more water flows into the river, so the channel gets wider. Two rivers may join together. A small river flowing into a larger river is called a **tributary**. Eventually each river ends at its **mouth**, that is, where it reaches the sea.

ACTION!

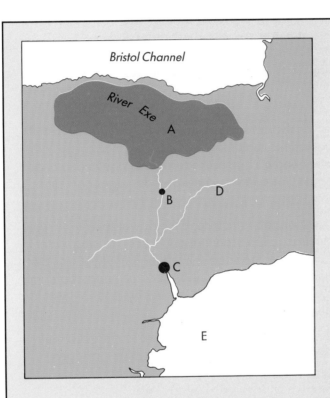

Bristol Channel

River Exe

A

B

D

C

E

Look at the sketch map of the River Exe. Find a map of Devon in an atlas.

1 Name area A, the high land where the source of the Exe is found.

2 Name the towns marked B and C. Which town is closer to the mouth?

3 Name the tributary marked D.

4 Name the sea area E into which the river Exe flows.

5 In which direction does the Exe flow?

Too much water!

Sometimes a river can carry so much water that it cannot all be contained in the river's channel. As more water is added the river 'bursts its banks' and floods the surrounding countryside. Most floods occur after a period of heavy rain when the amount of water entering the river is more than it can cope with. If rainwater reaches the river quickly then this could lead to an increased risk of flooding. The concrete and tarmac of towns and cities do not allow water to soak into the ground. Instead it runs into drains, which may ultimately empty into a river. So, more water reaches the river in less time. This could cause a flood.

The effects of flooding

When a river 'bursts its banks' the effect on the surrounding countryside can be devastating. The flood waters carry mud, stones and various items that have been washed away. When this water and mud mixture washes into people's homes it causes damage to personal possessions and the structure of the houses themselves. The water damages cars and anything in its path.

Sometimes small streams become raging torrents which have the power to uproot trees and wash away buildings. Bridges can trap fallen branches and trees, causing water to build up even more and increasing the effect of the flood still further. Farmland can be inundated and livestock threatened or crops destroyed. Roads become impassable and normal, everyday life is severely disrupted. In severe floods there is the possibility of loss of life with the increased risk of accidents.

When the flood waters drain away the effects remain. People have to clean up their houses, repairs have to be made to services such as roads, railway lines, bridges, drains, etc. before life can return to normal.

Flood prevention

Some places are particularly prone to flooding. These high risk areas are sometimes found in the middle of towns. If people and property are regularly affected by flood waters it may become feasible to protect the threatened area. Flood prevention schemes may involve building walls or embankments or even widening or dredging the river. The idea is that the water in the river will be quickly channelled away rather than flowing over its banks into the surrounding town. One such scheme can be found in Monmouth.

Case study: The Monmouth scheme

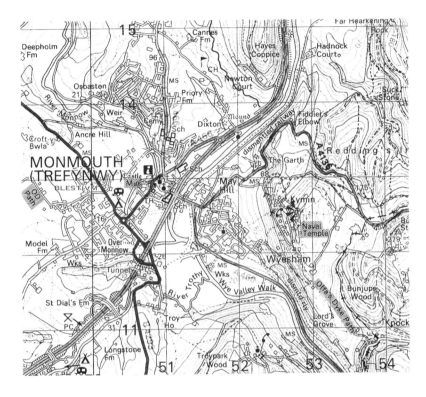

The river Wye as seen from Monmouth Bridge

Banking along the river Monnow

Monmouth has a long history of flooding. The local school and playing fields were regularly under water and the town centre itself has been flooded no less than seven times since 1910. Monmouth is particularly prone to flooding as the river Monnow joins the river Wye in the town. The commonest pattern of flooding is that the Monnow overflows first, followed between 18 to 36 hours later by the river Wye, thus causing a second flood in the town.

Part of the completed flood defence scheme

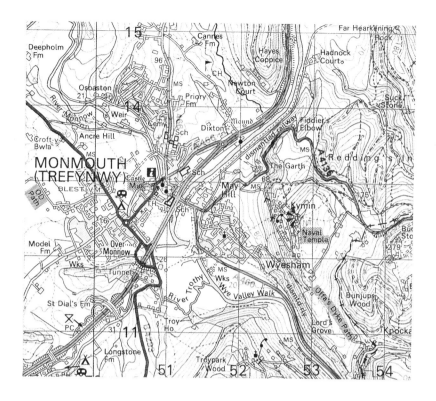

Considerable public anxiety was evident following the flood of 1979. This flood affected at least 190 commercial, industrial and residential properties. After a lengthy feasibility study and public enquiry the go-ahead was finally given for the £1.15 million scheme in July 1988, the work being completed in the spring of 1990.

What was done

The aim was to protect the town from the highest flood expected in one hundred years. The river Monnow had been widened in the 1930s and could not be widened again so the only alternative was the building of walls and embankments. Along the river Wye a small bank was constructed together with flood gates and flap valves (hinged flaps which open during times of flood, thus preventing water from reaching the town).

Monmouth's historical interest needed to be preserved

One problem that had to be overcome was that in Monmouth the immediate surroundings of the river were of special historical interest. 'The raising of walls and embankments for the flood alleviation scheme necessarily has an impact on the environment. In designing the works, the aim has been to construct defences that are both functional in an engineering sense, and yet sensitive to the environment in which they are built.'
(National Rivers Authority)

Storm hydrographs

The amount of water in a river is greatly affected by the total amount of rain over a period of time. A storm hydrograph helps us gauge whether a particular river will flood or not. This is a graph showing the amount and intensity of rainfall related to the amount of water flowing in the river (the **discharge**).

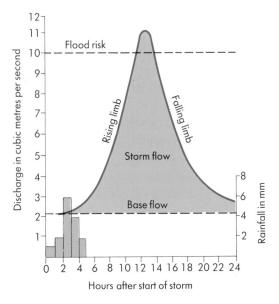

The amount of rainfall is shown as a bar graph and the discharge as a line graph. Notice how the amount of water in the river begins to rise soon after the rain starts. Water takes some time to flow over the land so the peak discharge comes after the peak rainfall. The time difference between the two is called the **lag**.

Notice how the base flow remains more or less constant. This is the groundwater entering the river. It shows what the river level would have been if it had not rained. Groundwater allows rivers to flow even when it has not rained for several weeks.

The area marked **storm flow** represents the extra amount of water in the river as a result of the storm. The river will only flood when the peak discharge line rises over the flood risk line.

As rain falls the river level will inevitably rise, but the rate at which it rises and, therefore, the risk of flooding, depend on a number of factors:

• Very heavy rain for a short period of time is more likely to cause a flood than the same amount of rain over a longer period of time.

• Some rocks do not allow water to soak in (they are **impermeable**) so water runs off the surface and quickly reaches the river. Some rocks soak up a lot of water so it takes a long time for the extra water to reach the river.

• In towns and cities drains and sewers allow storm waters to reach the river quickly so that downstream of a town the risk of flooding may be greater.

• Some rivers are very long so that the extra water is spread over a greater length, lessening the risk of flooding. Shorter rivers have less time to adjust to the extra water.

• Sometimes the surface may already be waterlogged. This again means that water will run off and quickly reach the river.

ACTION!

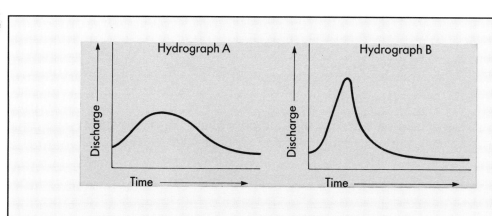

Look carefully at the two hydrographs.

1 Match each of these statements with the correct hydrograph:

permeable rock   impermeable rock   urban area   rural area
gentle rising limb   steep rising limb

2 Which hydrograph suggests the greater flood risk?
Explain your answer.

UNIT 7
Using water

SOURCES OF FRESH WATER

Water is essential for the modern way of life. Every one of us in Britain uses on average about 100 litres of clean, fresh water every day. Even more is used for farming, industry and recreation and the total amount used is increasing all the time. Changing lifestyles has led to more water being needed in the home, for things like automatic washing machines, dishwashers and garden sprinklers. To make one tonne of steel, 250 000 litres of water are needed.

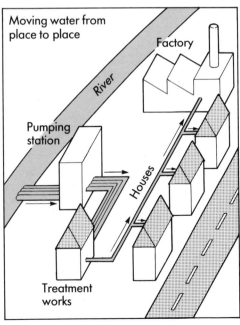

Irrigating farmland

Rainfall is free. The costs come when water has to be stored, transported and cleaned.

Costs for water uses:

Toilet flush 1p	Bath 8p
Shower 4p	Washing machine 13p
Dishwasher 6p	Hosepipe 54p per hour

Where does our water come from?

All our water originally falls as rain. Some of that rainwater is then stored in rocks as groundwater, or in rivers or reservoirs. It is from these that the water is taken, treated and pumped into our homes and factories.

A pumping station

Moving water from place to place

Factory
River
Pumping station
Houses
Treatment works

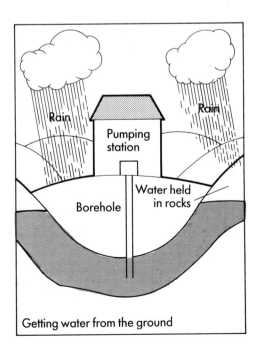

Rain
Pumping station
Rain
Water held in rocks
Borehole

Getting water from the ground

Maintaining supplies

We are very fortunate in this country that it rains quite a lot. This means we have a regular supply of water. But most rain falls in the mountains of the north and west, where demand is low. More water is needed in the south and east, where more people live and where there is more farmland. There is a limit to how much can be taken out of rivers and from the ground, so that means water has to be moved around the country.

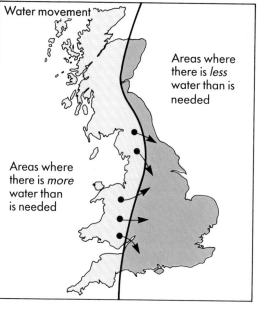

Water movement

Areas where there is *less* water than is needed

Areas where there is *more* water than is needed

In recent years water companies have had difficulty in maintaining regular supplies. The problem has been caused by:

- A series of warm, dry summers.
- Rain does not always fall where it is most needed.
- In warm weather more water is used – more gardens and parks have to be watered.
- In some areas up to 35% of water is lost through leaks, because water mains are very old.
- Increasing demand.

When there is a water shortage it is called a **drought**.
If more water is needed, why don't we build more reservoirs?

Conflict in the countryside! The need for water

Should we build a reservoir?

It is proposed to build a dam across the valley of a stream in a highland area. It will create a lake 7½ miles square in area, and provide the city 65 miles away (total population 600 000) with a regular supply of fresh water and some electricity. In doing so, it will drown a picturesque village including 12 houses, a church and a pub, and flood 2500 hectares of valuable farmland.

The valley before the dam is built

Artist's impression of how the valley will look after the dam is built

ACTION!

1 A scheme such as this often provokes different views from different people. Below are a list of comments and a list of people who said them. Match each comment to the correct person.

(a) 'Think of all the jobs that will be created.' Local farmer

(b) 'I don't want to live anywhere else.' Chairman of 'Damit', the construction company

(c) 'We must guarantee water supplies to everyone.' A conservationist

(d) 'Think of all the wildlife that will be destroyed.' A watersports enthusiast

(e) 'My family have worked this land for 150 years.' Manager of water company

(f) 'Think of the added attraction to tourists of fishing, sailing and windsurfing.' Local resident

2 Three of the above are for the scheme and three against. Which are which?

3 Deep, narrow mountain valleys are ideal locations for reservoirs. Give three reasons why this is so.

4 The alternative to building more reservoirs is to use water more efficiently. Suggest two ways in which we could cut down on the amount of water we use.

DIRTY WATER: EFFECTS AND SOLUTIONS

Many of the pollutants that reach our rivers and seas get there through carelessness *or* lack of concern for our environment *or* because the cost of pollution protection is too high. Pollution has far-reaching effects, but, given commitment, there *are* solutions to the problem.

ACTION!

Effects of pollution	Source of Pollution	Solutions
Fumes and rainwater mixing together cause acid rain. When it gets into rivers and lakes it kills fish and plants.		Cleaning equipment fitted to cooling towers.
Untreated sewage carries high levels of bacteria which can lead to disease.		Treat sewage more efficiently before it is dumped.
Nitrates in drinking water lead to stomach cancer and are dangerous for pregnant mothers.		Encourage organic farming, using crop rotation and natural fertilisers.
Farmyard waste is very toxic if allowed to reach water courses.		Government investment in recycling factories extracting reusable fertiliser from farmyard waste.
Rotting domestic rubbish produces dangerous gases. Water seeping through washes toxic chemicals into the river.		Encourage people to recycle their household waste, as the city of Sheffield has done.
Uncontrolled discharges from factories can kill aquatic life immediately.		Make individual firms pay heavy fines for pollution incidents or introduce high taxation for major polluters.

Warm water from power stations leads to a reduction in oxygen levels in water, which can kill fish.		Generate electricity using renewable sources of energy.
High concentration of exhaust gases leads to eye irritations and nausea, as well as acid rain.		Fit catalytic converters to all exhausts.

Look very carefully at the statements in the 'effects of pollution' and 'solutions' columns in the table above and the list of different types of pollution below. Copy out the table, writing the correct source of pollution in the correct box.

factory discharges   landfill seepage   acid rain   traffic fumes
farmyard slurry   nitrates   sewage disposal   power stations

Water pollution – the price of progress?

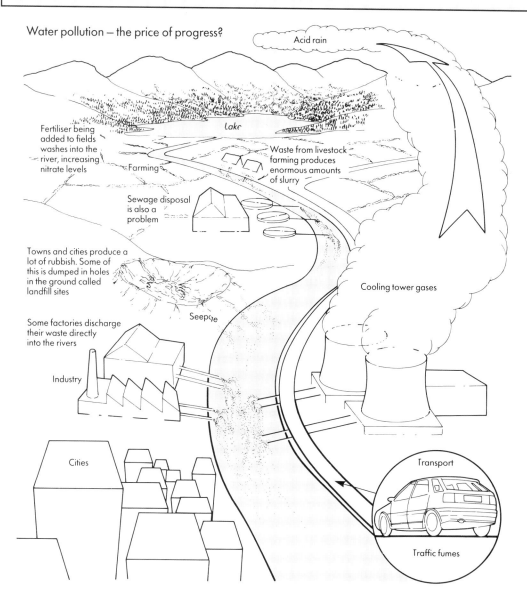

The North Sea: Europe's dustbin

The North Sea is rapidly becoming one of the most polluted parts of the ocean in the world. This is because the industrial countries which surround it have been dumping industrial waste and toxic chemicals in it for the past 100 years. This shallow sea is now beginning to show signs of the consequences of indiscriminate waste disposal.

The causes

Sewage sludge is pumped directly into the sea and so too is waste from industry.

The North Sea has some of the busiest shipping lanes in the world. Oil tankers illegally washing out their tanks cause oil pollution.

Ships dump many industrial waste products, or burn them at sea, hoping they dissolve in the sea water.

Several of Europe's major rivers drain into the North Sea. Each one carries its own cocktail of chemicals as a result of flowing through the industrial heartland of Europe.

The North Sea

Forth
Tyne
Tees
Humber
Thames
Scheldt
Rhine
Ems
Weser
Elbe

① ② ③ ④ ⑤ ⑥ ⑦ ⑧

ACTION!

1 Look at the table below. Draw a bar graph to show how much mercury is deposited in the North Sea each year by each river.

2 Use an atlas to name the eight countries which border the North Sea.

River pollution of the North Sea

River	Mercury (tonnes per year)	Cadmium (tonnes per year)	Nitrogen (thousand tonnes per year)	Phosphorus (thousand tonnes per year)
Forth	0.1	2.0	1	—
Tyne	1.4	1.3	1	0.2
Tees	0.6	0.6	2	0.2
Humber	0.7	3.5	41	0.6
Thames	1.1	1.5	31	0.1
Scheldt	1.0	7.4	62	7.0
Rhine	3.9	13.8	420	37.0
Ems	0.4	0.7	22	0.7
Weser	1.1	2.9	87	3.8
Elbe	7.3	8.4	150	12.0

From: The Environment (Collins)

Beaches around the North Sea have become heavily polluted. In 1989 only 22 of Britain's beaches were awarded the coveted EC Blue Flag for cleanliness. Many traditional tourist resorts failed the test.

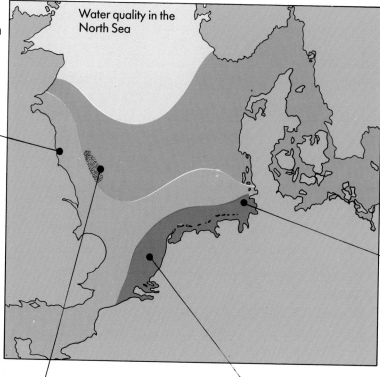

Water quality in the North Sea

Key:

Fair

Poor

Very poor

Extremely poor

Huge blooms of algae have grown, accelerated by the thousands of tonnes of fertiliser washed down rivers.

Marine life is affected. Many seals have died recently as a result of a 'mystery' virus.

Fish stocks are declining. Some of the fish that are caught show the effects of pollution – ulcers, cancerous growths, bulbous eyes, especially in flat fish like plaice which live on the sea bottom. 'Heavy' metals like mercury and cadmium do not dissolve in sea water so they sink to the bottom and build up in the sediment.

The solutions

Cleaning the North Sea is going to be a very difficult and expensive task. The first task is to get the eight nations to agree on how to do it and who will pay.

ACTION!

You have been asked by your local conservation group to write a letter to your Euro MP. In it you put forward a long-term plan of how to go about cleaning up the North Sea. Make some suggestions about the way the problems can be overcome. You may like to consider:

How could oil spillage be reduced?
How could industrial waste dumping be reduced?
Who will clean up the beaches?
What about marine wildlife?
Who will pay for the clean-up?

UNIT 8
Shaping the land

WEATHERING

All surfaces that are exposed to the weather are attacked by weathering. Metal rusts, roads crack, statues crumble, and rocks and buildings break up. Evidence of the effect of the weather can be seen all around.

Chemical weathering

Types of weathering

There are three types:

1 Physical weathering

This is where rocks are broken down into smaller and smaller particles. One way in which this happens is through freeze/thaw action. Water that has collected in cracks and hollows in the rock will freeze when temperatures fall below 0°C. As it does so it expands,

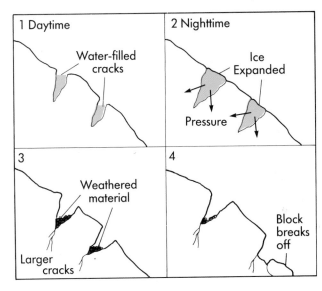

Physical weathering

increasing pressure on the rock. When it thaws the pressure is released. Repeated freezing and thawing causes the rock to weaken and crumble so eventually the crack becomes wider. Whole blocks of rock can break off in this way. Freeze/thaw action is commonest in mountain areas where temperatures fluctuate around 0°C for much of the year.

2 Chemical weathering

As rainwater falls through the air it becomes a very weak type of acid. When this acidic water comes into contact with rock it starts to dissolve it. The rate at which it dissolves depends on the type of rock. Limestone, for example, dissolves very quickly. Many buildings are built partly of limestone and the results of chemical weathering can clearly

A 'rusty' rock

be seen. Also, oxygen in the air can sometimes react with iron in the rocks so that they change to a deep red colour – the rocks actually become 'rusty'.

Pollution in towns and cities also increases chemical weathering. Evidence for this can be seen on blackened buildings.

Just like physical weathering, the presence of water is essential for chemical weathering to take place. The rate at which chemical weathering takes place depends on the temperature. The warmer it is, the more rapid the chemical decay.

3 Biological weathering

Animals and plants also cause weathering. Seeds may fall into cracks in the rocks. As water usually collects there, it forms ideal conditions for the seed to germinate and grow. As the plant develops its roots may push the rocks apart. Animals burrowing into the soil can also cause damage.

THE SOIL

A soil profile

The soil is very important to us all. The plants growing in the soil provide the air with oxygen, and ourselves and other plants and insects with food. Without the soil there would be no life on the land. The soil is vital for plants because it provides: stability for the plant to grow; a store of nutrients; a store of water.

The soil is made up of lots of different things which come from two basic sources – the **parent material** and **humus**. The parent material is the underlying rock which has broken down into stones, clay or sand. Humus is the name given to all the rotted plant matter – such as dead leaves and old roots – which provides the soil with its vital organic content. Also present in the soil are air, worms, bacteria and water, which all play vital roles.

Soil is formed over a very long period of time – several thousand years, in fact. The first stage in this very long process is when exposed rock is attacked by weathering. The rock is gradually broken down into smaller particles. The next stage involves plants beginning to root in the soil that has begun to form. The plant's roots and leaves add humus to the soil. These processes continue for hundreds of years before a mature soil of about 40cm is formed.

These are several different types of soil. A sandy soil has a gritty texture which drains well and does not feel sticky, even when wet. A clay soil has a smoother texture, does not drain well and is very sticky. A loam soil is a well-balanced mixture of sand, clay and humus.

EROSION, TRANSPORTATION AND DEPOSITION

The difference between weathering and erosion is that weathering rots the rocks and erosion removes them. Weathering prepares the rock for erosion. After rocks have been attacked by weathering they are then prone to erosion.

Erosion occurs where particles of rock or soil are:

* Washed away by a river.
* Removed by waves in the sea.
* Crushed under a glacier.
* Blown away by the wind.

Erosion occurs where nature is very powerful or is said to possess a lot of energy. This could be where:

* A river flows very fast.
* Large waves are whipped up by a storm and crash onto the coastline.
* Thick ice presses down on the Earth's surface.
* The wind is strong enough to pick up particles of rock.

After material has been 'picked up' it is **transported** or moved to another place. The distance covered may be small – for example, from the front of a beach to the back of the beach; or large – for example, hundreds or even thousands of miles down a river.

Eventually transported materials will be deposited or dumped. **Deposition** occurs where:

* A river flows slowly.
* The sea washes up gently against a beach.
* The ice of a glacier begins to melt.
* Areas are sheltered from the wind.

How rivers shape the land

All rivers flow from mountains to the sea and as they do so they have the ability to shape the land. Rivers use **energy** to erode, transport and deposit material. The amount of energy a river has depends on the steepness of the land over which it is flowing (because water always flows downhill, due to gravity) and how much water is in the river. Generally the steeper the land and the more water in the channel, the faster the river flows. When a river has a lot of energy, i.e. when it is flowing quickly, or after heavy rain, then it has the ability to erode its bed and banks. It can also transport eroded material more easily. When it loses energy it no longer has the ability to transport its materials, so deposition occurs. The amount of erosion varies considerably from day to day and season to season. Remember that rivers are 'lazy' – they find the easiest possible way to the sea.

A river erodes through:

Corrasion: Material carried along within the river crashes into the bed and banks, causing material to break off.

Attrition: Particles knocking together whilst being carried along by the river.

Abrasion: A common name to describe both corrasion and attrition.

Corrosion: River water dissolving some or all of the rocks over which it flows.

Hydraulic action: Air trapped in cracks and holes is compressed, which leads to weakening of material along the bed and banks of the river.

Cavitation: This occurs mainly in waterfalls where millions of bursting bubbles send out shock waves that weaken the rocks.

A river transports material by:

Suspension: Small particles, light enough to be carried along within the river. The amount of suspended material that can be carried depends on the speed of the river. After heavy rain many rivers turn brown with sediment.

Solution: Dissolved materials resulting from corrosion.

Traction: Larger rocks and pebbles cannot be lifted so they are rolled along the bed of the river.

Saltation: Particles jumping downstream.

Deposition occurs when a river starts losing its energy. Heavier particles get deposited first whilst light material will be transported as long as the river has enough energy. Eventually, this too will be dumped, although sometimes not until the river reaches its mouth. The river therefore sorts out material as it deposits.

Look carefully at the photograph. It shows that erosion, transportation and deposition can occur side by side in a river.

1 How does X show evidence of deposition?

2 How does Y show evidence of transportation?

3 How does Z show evidence of erosion?

Shapes created by rivers

As a river moves down its valley its character changes, and so too do the landforms which it creates.

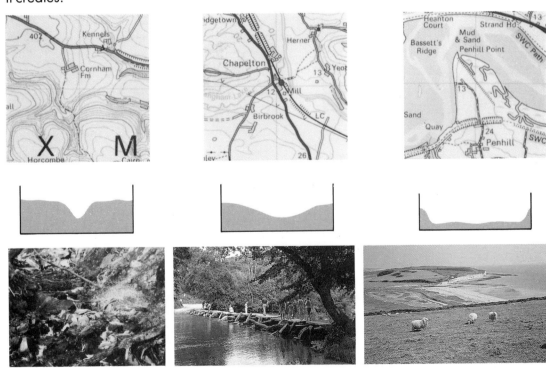

The upper course

In the upper course a river is usually small but flows very fast. Energy levels are high and the river cuts away at its bed. As it does so it quickly deepens its valley through 'downcutting' which creates a steep-sided V-shaped valley. Erosion is the dominant process.

Landforms found in the upper course

1 Waterfalls and gorges

One way in which a waterfall can occur is when hard rock lies over the top of softer rock. The softer rock is eroded more easily, which leaves the harder rock overhanging. Eventually, after undercutting has occurred, the harder rock collapses into the river. The waterfall retreats to a position further upstream. If this process happens several times then a steep-sided gorge is left downstream of the waterfall. This can be seen clearly at High Force waterfall on the River Tees.

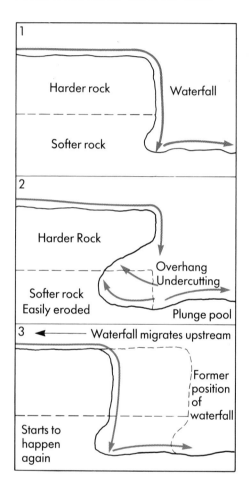

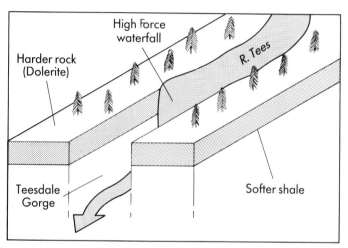

2 Interlocking spurs

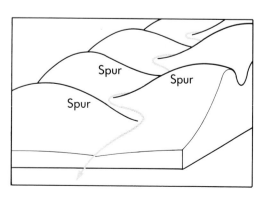

As the river starts to wind its way down its valley it creates a series of **interlocking spurs**. These are small hills that fit together neatly like the pieces of a jigsaw, around which the river flows.

The middle course

As a river moves down its valley a number of changes occur:

- The river gets wider as more and more tributaries join together.
- The valley sides become less steep, giving a much more open V-shape.
- Instead of the river eroding downwards into its bed, it begins to erode sideways into its banks which opens out the valley floor and a flood plain starts to develop.
- Erosion still occurs but there is also some deposition.
- The edges of the flood plain are marked by bluffs.

Landforms found in the middle course

1 Meanders

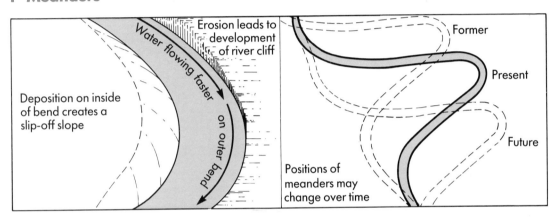

A river seldom flows in a straight line. As it wanders from side to side it creates loops, called meanders. Water travels faster on the outside of bends so the river erodes its banks, while on the inside of the bends deposition occurs in the slacker water.

Meanders are constantly changing and over time can actually move downstream.

A cross-section of a meander

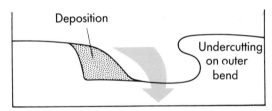

2 Flood plains

A flood plain is a flat area of land found on the floor of the valley, immediately next to a river. This is the area that is affected by flood waters after excessively heavy rain. It is formed by the river meandering from side to side, wearing away the valley's spurs. Flood plains are covered with layers of **alluvium** (the fine, muddy material spread by a river during floods).

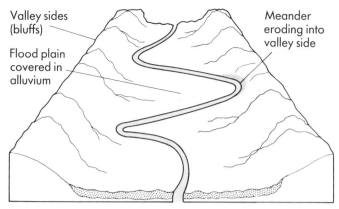

Valley sides (bluffs)

Flood plain covered in alluvium

Meander eroding into valley side

The lower course

As a river approaches its mouth more subtle changes occur in its character. The valley's V-shape is now so wide that the valley sides have all but disappeared. The river now winds its way slowly across a large flood plain. Deposition is now the dominant process.

In Britain most rivers are not long enough or large enough to develop the full-scale features found in the lower courses of many of the world's great rivers, such as the Mississippi. Instead many British rivers end their journeys to the sea in an estuary.

How the sea shapes the land

Just as rivers have the ability to create shapes in the landscape so too does the sea. As the sea washes up against the coastline it uses its energy to erode material from the land, transport it to another place and deposit it. The sea gains its energy from the wind. As the wind blows, the surface of the sea is whipped up into a series of waves. The amount of energy or power each wave possesses depends on:

the strength of the wind – the stronger the wind, the greater the wave;

how far the wave has travelled (the **fetch**) – waves that have travelled greater distances are usually more powerful;

how long the wind has been blowing for – the longer the time, the higher the wave.

Erosion will occur when powerful waves are allowed to strike at exposed parts of the coastline, e.g. a headland. Wave power is greater during times of storm when the wind is stronger.

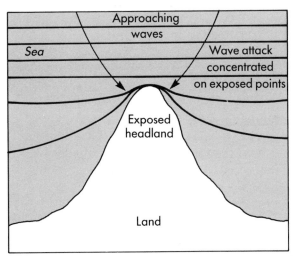

The sea erodes by:

Hydraulic action: air in cracks in the rock being compressed and quickly released by waves.

Abrasion: pebbles being thrown at the cliff face by the waves.

Attrition: pebbles rubbing against each other. This is why pebbles are smooth – all the sharp edges have been knocked off. You can hear attrition happening, when waves drag pebbles back towards the sea.

Corrosion: rocks being dissolved by sea water and removed in solution.

Material is **transported** along the coast by waves and the currents in the sea. The main process of transportation is **long shore drift**. Waves rarely strike the coastline directly, so instead, waves and the material they carry are washed in at an angle. Gravity pulls the material back towards the sea at right angles, only for the next wave to move it forward at an angle. The result is that material moves along the coast. **Groynes** are sometimes placed on popular beaches to stop this happening.

Long shore drift

A pebble starting at point X will eventually end up at point Y, due to long shore drift.

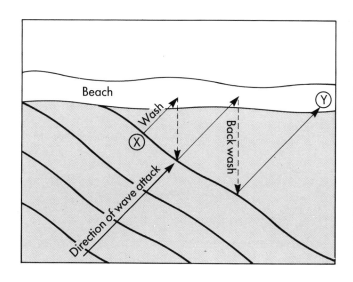

Groynes are wooden fences built out into the sea. They are designed to stop valuable beach material being totally removed. They also break up the waves' energy during times of storm.

Deposition occurs in sheltered areas along the coast where the waves lose energy. This can happen when (i) the wind dies down, or (ii) in areas of deeper water, or (iii) where the shape of the coastline causes the waves to bend or become refracted.

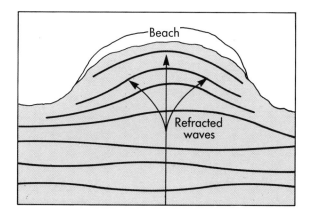

Refraction causes waves to lose energy, therefore they have less power.

ACTION!

1 Why is area A prone to erosion?

2 Explain where the beach material B came from, how it got there and why it was deposited at that particular location.

3 Why would the local council in charge of a popular tourist beach want to construct and maintain a series of groynes?

4 Explain why pebbles on a beach are rounded.

5 'Hydraulic action causes more damage to a coastline than it does to a river valley.' Why do you think this is so?

Case study: The North Devon coast

Cliffs and wave-cut platforms

The sea can only erode between the levels of the highest and the lowest tides. If the land is high and the coastline is open to wave attack then cliffs are likely to form. The sea begins by cutting a notch between high water mark (HWM) and low water mark (LWM). As erosion continues the notch becomes so large that the overhanging rocks collapse into the sea. A cliff results. As erosion continues to eat into the land the cliff moves further and further back. As it does so it leaves a flat area in front of the cliff called a wave-cut platform.

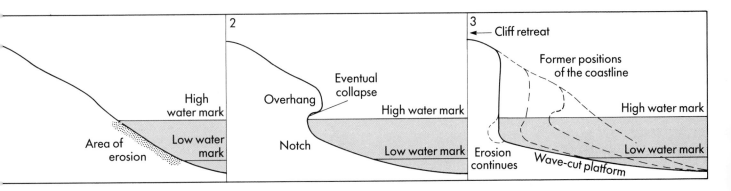

The cliffs along the North Devon coast are very high and steep. This suggests that rapid erosion is occurring. The base of the cliff is being cut away so quickly that the top of the cliff does not have enough time to wear down through weathering. The most dramatic cliffs form in hard rocks, as softer ones simply collapse and crumble.

The formation of stacks

Headlands are masses of rock that are surrounded on three sides by the sea. As they 'stick out' from the coastline they are exposed to the full force of wave erosion.

The sea concentrates its attack on a weak point in the headland (a fault or a weak joint) and carves out a cave. If there is a weakness on the other side of the headland then two caves may form. After further erosion the two caves join up to form a natural arch. Sometimes, as a result of hydraulic action, air forces its way to the surface, up through the roof of the cave, forming a blow hole. As erosion continues the roof of the cave collapses, leaving an isolated pillar of rock called a **stack**. Stacks themselves erode in time leaving a stump, visible only at low tide.

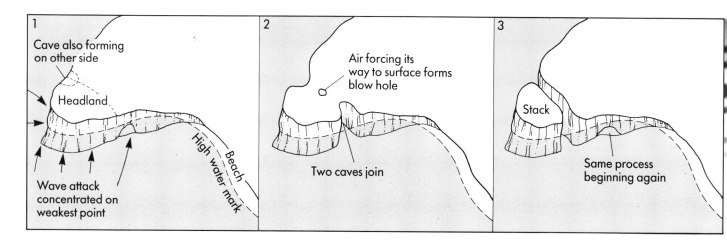

A natural arch

Stacks

ACTION!

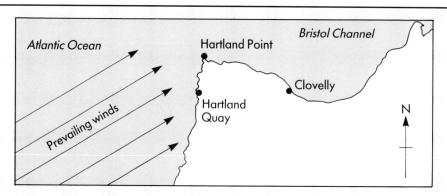

1 Look at the sketch map of part of the North Devon coast. Give two pieces of map evidence which indicate that the coastline south of Hartland Point is likely to be affected by erosion.

2 Hartland Point is a notorious graveyard for ships. How do you account for this?

3 How does the photograph of the waterfall near Clovelly (below) suggest that this coastline is eroding?

Coastal deposition

Eroded material is moved along the coastline by long shore drift until it reaches deeper water, where it is deposited. This may be as a beach at the head of a bay or as a **spit**. A spit forms where there is a sudden change in the direction of the coastline. Material moving along the coast is deposited and this gradually builds up above sea level. As more and more material is added the spit grows into the sea. Wave action sometimes causes the end of the spit to become hooked. Further deposition and silting occurs behind the spit so that afterwards the area becomes an area of salt marsh.

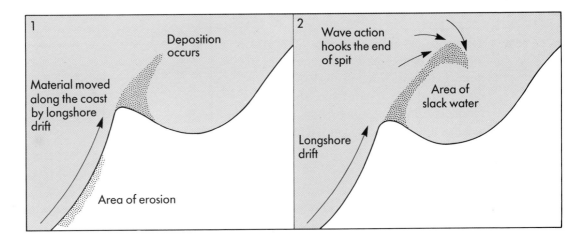

ACTION!

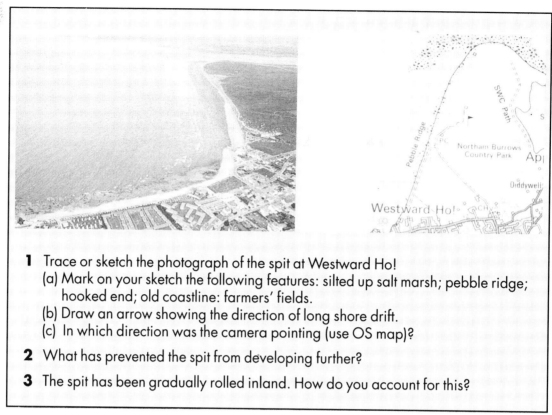

1 Trace or sketch the photograph of the spit at Westward Ho!
   (a) Mark on your sketch the following features: silted up salt marsh; pebble ridge; hooked end; old coastline: farmers' fields.
   (b) Draw an arrow showing the direction of long shore drift.
   (c) In which direction was the camera pointing (use OS map)?

2 What has prevented the spit from developing further?

3 The spit has been gradually rolled inland. How do you account for this?

Man's response to the changing coastline

Lonely Victory of Outpost in War of the Waves

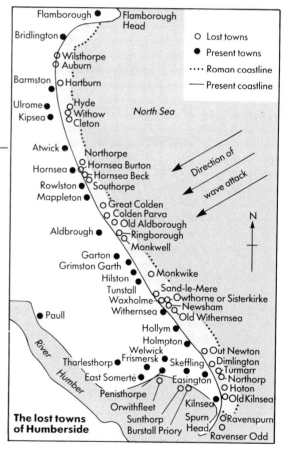

The lost towns of Humberside

Forty yards from a sign warning of coastal erosion and a barrier to stop unwary motorists, Cliff Lane ends, appropriately, in a sheer 60-foot drop to the beach.

This 30-mile stretch of the Humberside coast suffers the worst erosion in Europe and is retreating at a rate of more than six feet a year.

Time and tides have taken their toll of 29 villages over the past two centuries. The last house in Old Aldborough, the latest victim, disappeared only 10 years ago. The only reminders of the hotel, pub, shop, village store and handful of houses are the pictures in a local museum.

Mappleton was set to join the roll call of doomed villages. Ponderosa Cottage is perched precariously near the edge, its owners long gone, boarded up until it collapses into the chilly brown waters eating away the sheer face of clay. In Mappleton they measure the inroads of the North Sea by watching the tarmac of Cliff Lane falling away.

But now it appears Mappleton has been saved from a watery grave. Bargeloads of granite are to be brought from Norway to build a coastal defence costing £2 million. The shipments mark the end of a two-year campaign by locals to save the village.

Dot Meggitt has lived in the lane for 35 years. When she arrived the sea was more than a quarter of a mile away. It is now less than 60 yards from her home, which is the next target for the relentless tides.

She said: 'When the tide is in I can hear the waves rocking the house. The only consolation is that by the time the sea arrives I will probably be under the sod. This is England that is disappearing.'

The village names live on out in the North Sea, where oil rigs have been named after them. But as Mrs Meggitt said: 'The last thing we want is for Mappleton to be just another oil rig.'

It would cost £250 million to shore up the entire coastline, and the authorities say that when time is up for a village or farmstead it is left to nature.

The saviour of Mappleton, which was mentioned in the Domesday Book and dates from Saxon times, is the B1242 Hornsea to Withernsea coastal road. If the village disappeared, so would the road and the cost of re-routing the vital link makes protecting Mappleton economically viable.

It is good news for the 100 villagers. With the backing of the local Holderness District Council they have obtained government and Humberside County Council grants to pay for the bulk of the protection work.

The scheme will encourage greater erosion to the south, creating bays in the drearily straight coastline which could benefit the tourist trade.

From:
The Observer,
21 October 1990

Look at all the information in the photograph and map and read the article carefully before answering these questions:

1 Suggest two pieces of evidence to explain why this coastline is eroding so rapidly.

2 Erosion along the coastline has been a problem for centuries. What evidence supports this statement?

3 Why should Norwegian granite be used to protect the coastline?

4 (a) What is meant by 'economically viable'?
   (b) Why is protecting Mappleton 'economically viable'?

5 What 'benefits' could be brought to the area if the coastal defences were built?

6 (a) Why do you think the cost of building coastal defences is so great?
   (b) Why are they not a long-term option?

UNIT 9
Weather and climate in Britain

WEATHER MATTERS

The weather affects us all in some way. Did you need to take a raincoat to school today?

Will it be hot enough to go to the beach at the weekend?

Will there be enough snow to go sledging?

These are some of the many questions we ask when looking at the weather. Some people's jobs are directly affected by the weather — for example, farmers, builders or ice cream vendors.

Extremes of weather may lead to drought or flooding. Strong winds cause storm damage and heavy snow can block roads or even cut off whole villages.

The main feature of the British weather is that it is very changeable. It is the job of the weather forecaster to try and predict what the weather will be like in a few days' time.

1 How are the following occupations affected by the weather:
   (a) lifeguard on a beach; (b) fisherman/woman; (c) gardener;
   (d) street market trader?

2 Listen to the weather forecast for one week and make a note of how accurate
   each forecast is.

MICROCLIMATES

We all know that the weather changes frequently, but not so obvious are the subtle differences that occur in our immediate surroundings. The temperature at any particular place will depend on a number of factors:

Is it in the shade, or direct sunlight?
Is it sheltered from the breeze or exposed?
Is it on a surface that reflects or absorbs heat?

Buildings, man-made surfaces and vegetation (or lack of it) affect not only the temperature but also the strength of the wind and the amount of rainfall received. The word **microclimate** is used to describe small-scale changes in the weather.

ACTION!

Five groups of children carried out some fieldwork on a hot summer's day when the sun was high in the sky. Their task was to measure the temperature at the five different locations indicated on the map below. Starting at different points, the groups visited each of the sites in turn. Here are their results:

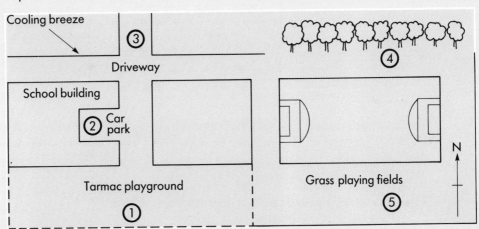

	Site 1	Site 2	Site 3	Site 4	Site 5
Group A	24°	26°	19°	22°	22°
Group B	23°	25°	20°	22°	20°
Group C	24°	28°	21°	22°	22°
Group D	24°	25°	17°	21°	20°
Group E	25°	26°	20°	23°	21°

Temperatures measured in degrees Celsius

1 Work out the average temperature for each site.

2 At which site was (a) the highest and (b) the lowest temperature recorded?

3 Which site had the greatest temperature range (difference between highest and lowest)?

4 Account for the variations in temperature between sites and within sites.

Fieldwork/enquiry

Measure the temperature of at least five sites around your school or garden. Wait for a sunny day and choose your sites carefully. Select a range of positions – some in shade, others in sunshine, some near buildings, others out in the open. Note the wind direction, if any.

Afterwards, look at the data you have collected and account for any differences.

TEMPERATURES ACROSS BRITAIN

Temperatures vary from place to place, from day to day and from season to season. Altitude, latitude and wind direction can all affect how warm or cold it is. The sea also plays a very important role.

Lines on a map joining places of the same average temperatures are called **isotherms**.

July isotherms

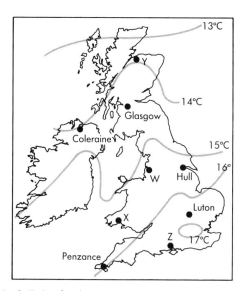

Temperatures during July fall the further north you go. This means that on average, southern England will be warmer than Scotland. In southern Britain the sun is much higher in the sky, so the sun's energy is more intense. The sea is colder than the land, so coastal areas are usually cooler than places inland.

The sea keeps summer temperatures down.

January isotherms

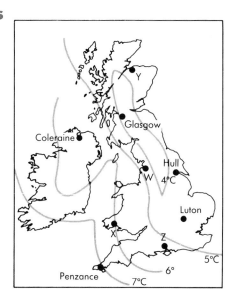

104

During January a warm ocean current, the North Atlantic Drift, allows warm air to pass over Britain. Temperatures are kept up so that much of Britain experiences mild winters.

Look at the map. Notice how temperatures fall from west to east, ie the further away you get from the ocean the colder the temperature.

The sea keeps winter temperatures up.

ACTION!

Use both isotherm maps to answer these questions:

1 Are these statements true or false?
(a) Luton has an average July temperature greater than 17°C.
(b) Penzance has an average January temperature greater than 7°C.
(c) Glasgow has an average January temperature less than 4°C.
(d) Both Coleraine and Glasgow are warmer than Hull during July.

2 Use the maps above and the table below to identify the places marked W, X, Y and Z.

Place	Average July temperature	Average January temperature	Letter
Bournemouth	16–17°C	5–6°C	
Pembroke	15–16°C	6–7°C	
Inverness	13–14°C	3–4°C	
Blackpool	15–16°C	4–5°C	

3 (a) Explain why Coleraine is cooler than Hull during July but warmer than Hull during January.
(b) Explain why the area to the south of Luton is the warmest part of Britain during July.
(c) Describe and account for the shape of the 6°C isotherm for January.

RAINFALL ACROSS BRITAIN

The British Isles receive a lot of rain. Usually the air passing over Britain comes from the south-west or west. As it passes over the Atlantic Ocean it picks up moisture through evaporation. By the time it reaches land the air is wet.

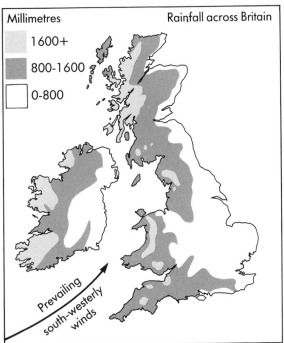

Millimetres   Rainfall across Britain

1600+

800–1600

0–800

Prevailing south-westerly winds

Not everywhere in Britain receives the same amount of rain. As the map shows, western Britain is much wetter than eastern Britain. One reason is because the land is much higher in the west (see Unit 1). Generally, the more mountainous the land, the wetter the weather (see 'relief rainfall', below).

What causes the rain?

Rain occurs where air is forced to rise. As it does so, it cools and condensation occurs, so clouds form. In western Britain the air is forced to rise because of the shape of the land. **Relief** rainfall results.

Relief rainfall

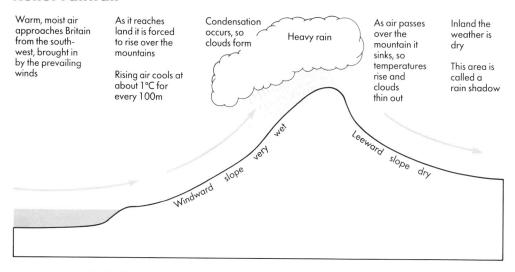

Warm, moist air approaches Britain from the south-west, brought in by the prevailing winds

As it reaches land it is forced to rise over the mountains

Rising air cools at about 1°C for every 100m

Condensation occurs, so clouds form

Heavy rain

As air passes over the mountain it sinks, so temperatures rise and clouds thin out

Inland the weather is dry

This area is called a rain shadow

Windward slope very wet

Leeward slope dry

Frontal rainfall

A front occurs where warm air meets cold air. The warm air is forced to rise over the cold air and as it does so, it cools, condenses and forms clouds. Eventually, it will start to rain. Fronts are a very common feature of the British weather.

Look at the diagram. Notice that there is a **warm front** and a **cold front.** The cold front rises more steeply and usually brings heavy rain. The clouds are thicker because the air is forced to cool quickly. The warm front rises less steeply, so more of the sky is covered with cloud.

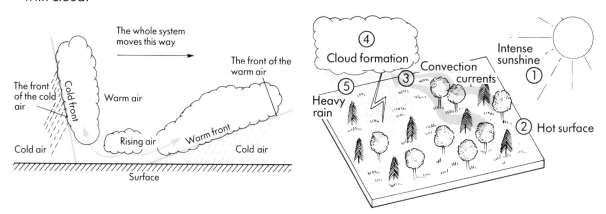

The whole system moves this way

The front of the cold air

Cold front

Warm air

The front of the warm air

Rising air

Warm front

Cold air

Cold air

Surface

Cloud formation ④

Convection currents

Intense sunshine ①

⑤ Heavy rain ③

② Hot surface

Convectional rain

Convectional rain is associated with very hot, humid weather, so it only rarely occurs in Britain. It happens when the Earth gets so hot that the air immediately above the surface is forced to rise. As it rises it cools, condensation occurs and clouds form. Eventually, very heavy rain falls, often accompanied by thunder and lightning. In some parts of the tropics this type of rain occurs nearly every day, usually during the afternoon.

WHAT WILL THE WEATHER BE LIKE TOMORROW?

Forecasting the weather is a very difficult job. Even today, with weather satellites and expensive computers, forecasters get it right only on about seven out of ten occasions. The main reason for this is that the atmosphere is always moving in different directions and it is sometimes difficult to predict which way the air will move.

Pressure gives us a good indication of what the weather will be like for the next few days. Basically, there are two types of pressure.

Air is pressing down on the land surface

This brings fine weather, as clouds do not form

High pressure

Air rises from the land. As it does so, clouds form and eventually it may rain

Low pressure

Weather associated with high pressure: anticyclones

High pressure cells are called **anticyclones.** They are stable, which means that the same weather may last for a few weeks at a time. An anticyclone during the summer brings fine, hot, sunny weather, but during the winter an anticyclone means fog and very cold temperatures with freezing conditions, but often with clear skies.

Lines joining places of the same pressure are called **isobars**. When isobars are far apart it means gentle winds. If isobars are closely packed together it means strong winds and gales.

High pressure during July

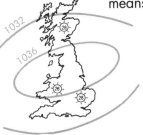

Summer

High pressure during January

Winter

ACTION!

1 Look at the information above. Can you see two similarities and two differences between an anticyclone in July and an anticyclone in January?

2 What can isobars tell us about the weather?

3 Look at the weather forecast for tomorrow. Are there any 'highs' on the chart? If so, make a note of the forecast. Is the weather forecast the same as you would expect?

Weather associated with low pressure: depressions

Low pressure cells are called **depressions**. They bring cloud, rain and, in many cases, strong winds. Air spins around the depression and is gradually sucked into the centre where it rises and forms clouds.

In a depression warm air gets trapped between two areas of colder air. The boundary between the warm and cold air is called a **front**. It is along the front that the heaviest rain occurs (see page 106).

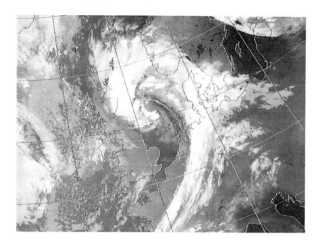

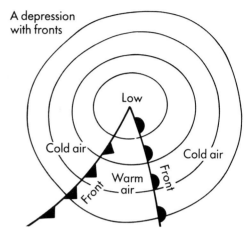

A depression with fronts

It usually takes two to three days for a depression to pass over the British Isles. During that time the weather can be very changeable, usually following a sequence.

A depression crossing Britain

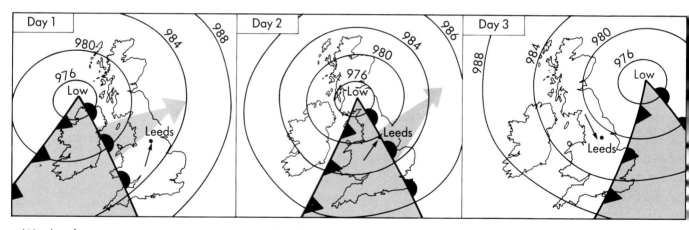

Weather: fine
Wind: from the south
Temperature: mild

Weather: heavy rain
Wind: from the south-west
Temperature: rises

Weather: showers
Wind: from the north-west
Temperature: drops

ACTION!

Look at the maps above.

1 How do you account for the heavy rain in Leeds on day 2?

2 Why does the temperature change from day to day?

3 Why does the wind keep on changing direction?

THE DIFFERENCE BETWEEN WEATHER AND CLIMATE

The **weather** of an area describes the day to day variations in the atmosphere, whereas the **climate** of a place is the average weather taken over the past 30 years. The climate suggests the sort of weather you may expect.

For example, the climate suggests that Cardiff has, on average, 13 rainy days in every December but the bar graph below shows what actually happened between 1961–90.

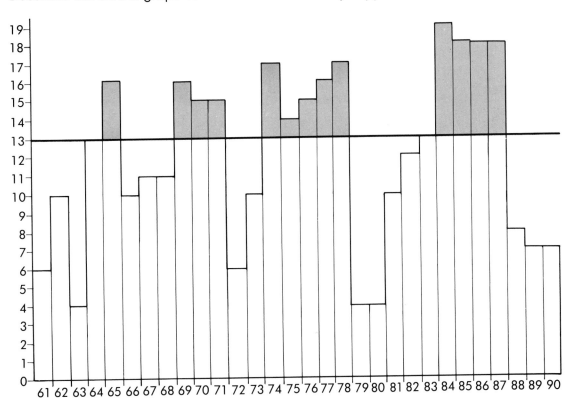

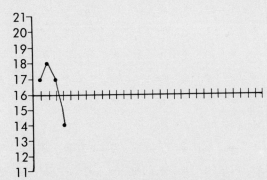

ACTION!

Look at the figures below, which show the maximum July temperature in Manchester for 1990:

Day	1	2	3	4	5	6	7	8	9	10	11	12	13	14	15	16	17	18	19	20	21	22	23	24	25	26	27	28	29	30	31
°C	17	18	17	14	14	13	13	11	21	20	21	20	21	15	15	16	16	17	18	16	16	20	21	18	15	14	14	14	15	16	16

1. Copy and complete the line graph above using the figures in the table.

2. Shade in red the part of the graph which shows temperatures above average.

3. Shade in blue the part of the graph which shows temperatures below average.

4. Was July 1990 warmer than or cooler than average in Manchester? Justify your answer.

IS BRITAIN'S CLIMATE CHANGING?

The late 1980s and 1990s have seen several dramatic weather events. 1987, 1988 and 1990 were three of the warmest years on record, with long periods without rain and sweltering summer temperatures. 1987 and 1990 also saw major storms which caused millions of pounds worth of damage to buildings as well as uprooting millions of trees. Are these the first signs of our changing climate? Recent scientific evidence has suggested that the whole planet is getting warmer. This has been called the **greenhouse effect**.

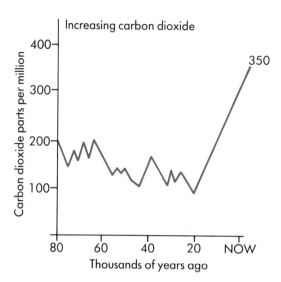

The greenhouse effect is the result of the way we live today. One of the main problems is that too much carbon dioxide is being pumped into the atmosphere. Carbon dioxide controls the heat balance of the earth. It allows heat from the sun in, but does not allow it to escape again. Heat is trapped in the atmosphere, so temperatures rise.

What carbon dioxide does to the atmosphere

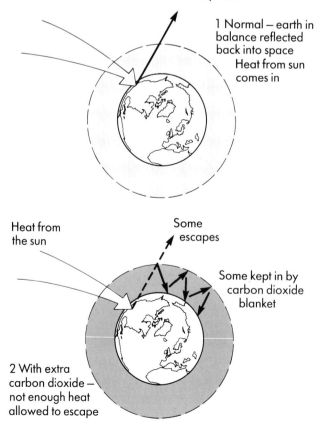

What causes the problem?

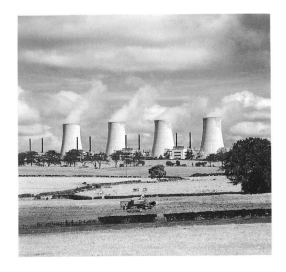

A coal-fired power station

Destroying the rainforest

Carbon is stored in the ground as coal, oil and gas. When we burn these fossil fuels carbon dioxide is released into the atmosphere.

Trees absorb carbon dioxide, so helping to maintain a balance. Cutting down forests upsets that balance. The problem is increased by burning fallen trees – more carbon dioxide gets into the atmosphere.

What problems will a warmer climate bring?

Nobody really knows what will happen if our world becomes warmer. Some of the effects could be alarming.

What the scientists say

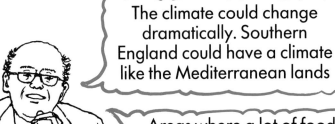

In Britain droughts during the summer and violent storms during the winter could become commonplace

The climate could change dramatically. Southern England could have a climate like the Mediterranean lands

A warmer Earth could cause ice caps and glaciers to melt so sea levels would rise

Areas where a lot of food is grown now could become deserts – where would we grow our food?

ACTION!

1 Use an atlas to locate the following cities. These are some of the most populated cities in the world. Which of them would be threatened if sea levels rose? London; New York; Calcutta; Mexico City; Tokyo; Jakarta; Cairo; Lagos; Paris; Seoul.

2 The map of Britain shows the lowland areas under threat from rising sea levels. Find a map of Britain in your atlas and fit the correct name to each arrow.

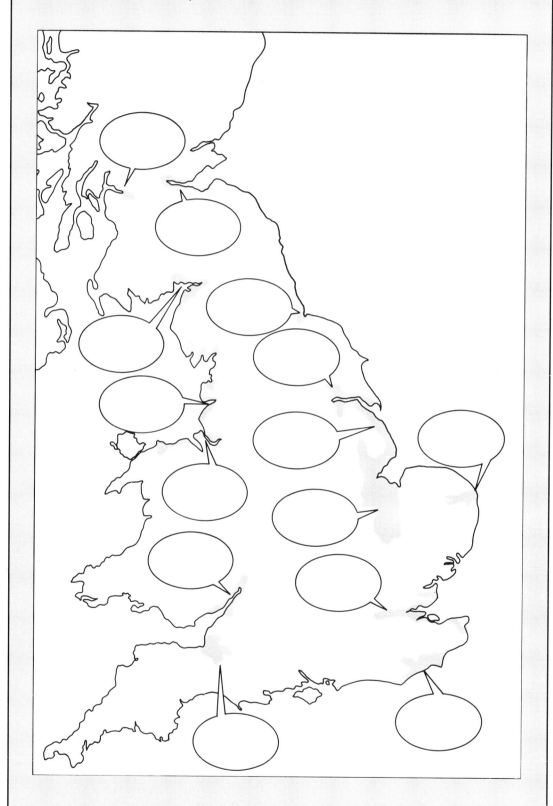

3 List four ways in which individuals can reduce the Greenhouse Effect.

UNIT 10
World climate and vegetation

FACTORS AFFECTING CLIMATE

The climate of an area depends on:

Nearness to the Equator: The Equator receives the maximum amount of heat and sunlight and so is generally warmer than elsewhere.

Height above sea level: Temperatures fall by 6°C per 1000 metre rise. Mountains are also wetter than low-lying areas.

Distance from the sea: The sea keeps summer temperatures down and winter temperatures up. Coastal areas are also much wetter than inland areas.

Direction of prevailing winds: Winds blowing across the sea bring cloud and rain.

Ocean currents: Ocean currents can raise or lower temperatures considerably, depending on whether they are hot or cold.

Plants respond to the climate, so it plays an important role in determining the type of vegetation found at a particular spot. All plants need sunlight, warmth, nutrients and water in order to survive, so where these are found in abundance, we find a large variety of plants and dense vegetation – e.g. the hot, wet rainforests. Where one of the factors is missing, then only a few specialist plants will be able to survive, so the vegetation cover will be sparse – e.g. the hot deserts.

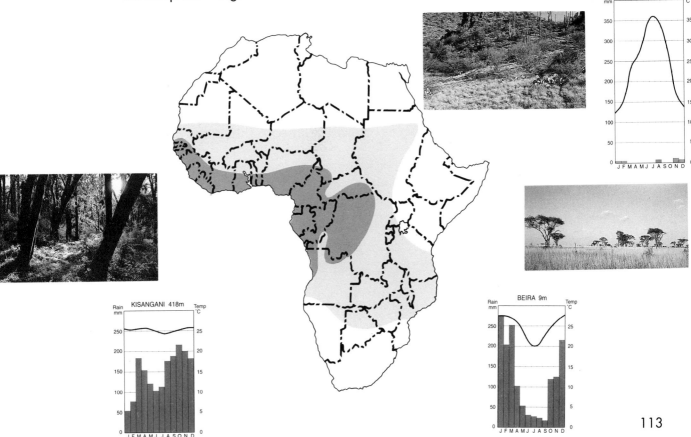

113

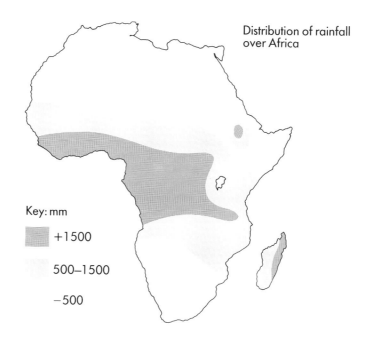

Distribution of rainfall over Africa

Key: mm

+1500

500–1500

–500

The climate changes very gradually from place to place and so too does the vegetation. For example, in Africa we can see a gradual change from the dense tropical forest around the Equator, to the tropical grassland and savannah, of the great African plains, to the vegetation-free hot deserts of the north and south-west.

AFRICA: NATURAL VEGETATION

ACTION!

> **1** Look at each of the photographs in the natural vegetation map (see previous page) and describe the vegetation shown in each one.
>
> **2** Identify four differences in the climate of each area.
>
> **3** Compare the natural vegetation map with the distribution of rainfall map. What relationship is suggested?

THE RAINFOREST

The main features of the climate ot the rainforest are that it is always hot and wet there. It is always hot because the sun is directly overhead. This means that the sun's rays are very strong.

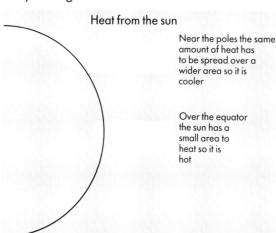

Heat from the sun

Near the poles the same amount of heat has to be spread over a wider area so it is cooler

Over the equator the sun has a small area to heat so it is hot

It is always wet because the intense heat causes convectional rain (see page 106). It rains nearly every day, often with thunder and lightning.

The warmth and moist air create ideal conditions for plants to grow. The vegetation is therefore very dense, with huge numbers of different types of plants (so much so that new species are being discovered every day). The tops of the trees form a continuous **canopy** so that the forest floor cannot be seen from the air. There is intense competition for light so that the trees grow tall and straight. The forest is so dense that very little light reaches the forest floor. There are no seasons, so that each individual tree flowers and sheds its leaves at different times of the year. The forest, therefore, seems evergreen. The vegetation grows in three distinct layers.

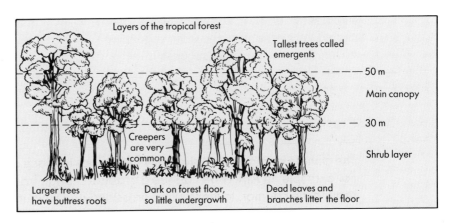

Layers of the tropical forest

Tallest trees called emergents

50 m

Main canopy

30 m

Shrub layer

Creepers are very common

Larger trees have buttress roots

Dark on forest floor, so little undergrowth

Dead leaves and branches litter the floor

ACTION!

1 Answer true or false to these statements:
(a) the Equator receives more of the sun's energy than Britain;
(b) frontal rainfall is common in the rainforest;
(c) it is more likely to rain in the morning than in the afternoon in a rainforest;
(d) September is the beginning of winter in the rainforest;
(e) jungle is another word to describe the vegetation in a rainforest.

2 Use a dictionary or encyclopaedia to find out the meaning of the following words:
undergrowth   lianas   epiphytes   parasites

3 Many of the tallest trees have 'buttress roots'. Why do you think these are important for the trees?

4 (a) Tropical hardwoods are very valuable. Why?
(b) Which of the following are tropical hardwoods?

oak   ebony   pine   mahogany   rosewood   beech   teak   walnut
elm   plywood

TROPICAL GRASSLANDS

The main feature of the climate of the tropical grasslands, or **savannahs** as they are sometimes called, is that there are two distinct seasons. The rainy, wet season comes during the summer when the overhead sun triggers convectional rain. 95% of all rain can fall in just four months. The dry season is very dry indeed, with severe drought conditions existing for most of the time. Both seasons are very hot.

These extremes in the availability of water makes life very difficult for plants. Trees find it difficult to cope with the drought, so only a few are found scattered across the plains. Thorny bushes and shrubs are more common, as their thick outer skins and needles for leaves cut down on water loss during the dry season. The main vegetation cover, as the name might suggest, is tall grass. During the wet season the grass is green and lush, but when drought conditions exist it turns into a golden carpet. Fires have always been common on the savannah, due to natural occurrences and man's activities, so many trees have thick barks to protect themselves against burning.

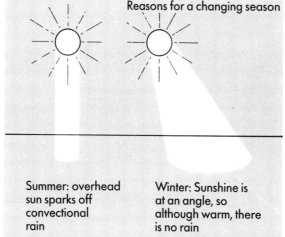

Reasons for a changing season

Summer: overhead sun sparks off convectional rain

Winter: Sunshine is at an angle, so although warm, there is no rain

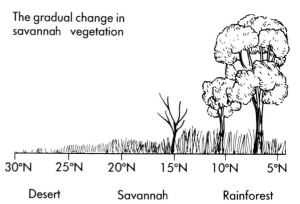

The gradual change in savannah vegetation

30°N 25°N 20°N 15°N 10°N 5°N

Desert   Savannah   Rainforest

ACTION!

1 What is the main difference between the climate of the rainforest and that of the savannah?

2 Give two ways in which savannah plants are adapted to drought conditions.

3 How do you account for the gradual change in the quantity of vegetation shown in the diagram above?

HOT DESERTS

The main features of the hot desert regions, or **arid lands** as they are sometimes called, are the searing heat and the lack of rainfall. They are the hottest, as well as the driest, places on Earth. During the day temperatures often exceed 50°C. At night, under cloudless skies, temperatures fall to around freezing. Rainfall is unreliable and infrequent and when it does come it often falls as torrential downpours.

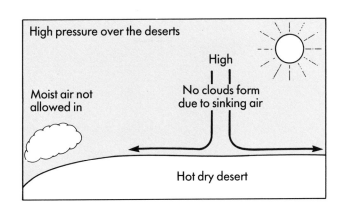

The reason why deserts are so dry is that they are usually covered with high pressure. This means that air is pressing down on the Earth's surface, so winds blow off the land towards the sea. Rain-bearing winds are not allowed to penetrate inland.

Plants find it very difficult to survive in such difficult conditions, therefore only a few specialist plants can be found in these hot dry regions and even then they are usually well spaced out. Most plants are succulents (store water) and have thick waxy skins to protect themselves from the sun. They have sharp needles or thorns which cut down on water loss. They have long roots which reach deep down to the groundwater. Seeds can lie dormant for many years waiting for the rains to bring them to life. After rain the desert is seen to bloom, as each plant takes advantage of the moisture.

ACTION!

Match the phrase on the left with its correct ending:

Desert plants are well spaced out because of	so temperatures fall rapidly.
Clouds are not allowed to form in deserts because	plants need to conserve water and nutrients.
During the night radiation is allowed to escape into space	descending air creates high pressure.
Growth rates in deserts are so slow because	they don't know when the rains will come again.
The main limiting factor for growth in desert regions	the competition for water.
Plants can produce seeds very quickly because	is the lack of water.

UNIT 11
Population

DISTRIBUTION OF POPULATION

At present there are over 5 billion people living on Earth and by the end of the century this will have increased to over 6 billion. Nearly half of all the people that have ever lived are alive today.

However, as the map shows, the world's population is not spread evenly across the globe. In fact, half of all peoples occupy only one twentieth of the land surface. Human beings can only live where conditions are right for life, so people are attracted to the most suitable areas. Few live in less favourable regions, as survival would prove difficult for large numbers of people.

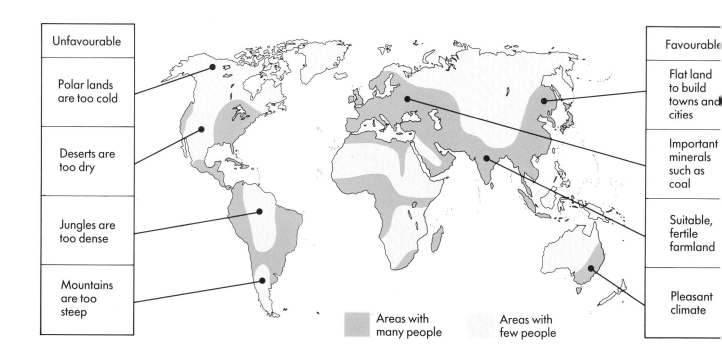

| Unfavourable |
| Polar lands are too cold |
| Deserts are too dry |
| Jungles are too dense |
| Mountains are too steep |

Areas with many people

Areas with few people

| Favourable |
| Flat land to build towns and cities |
| Important minerals such as coal |
| Suitable, fertile farmland |
| Pleasant climate |

The number of people living in an area is called the **population density**. It is worked out by dividing the total population by the total area, e.g.

The population density of the UK:

$$\frac{\text{Population}}{\text{Area}} = \frac{57\,080\,000}{245\,000 \text{ square km}} = 233 \text{ people per square km}$$

The UK is quite densely populated, but compare it to Hong Kong which has a population density of 14 073 per sq mile. Most cities have a much higher density of population than rural areas.

Case study: The population of Egypt

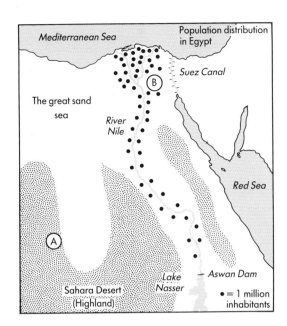

Egypt is a large country in North Africa. It has an area of 1 001 000 km² and a total population of 57 million. Much of the country is desert, except for a narrow strip of land on either side of the River Nile.

ACTION!

Look at all the information outlined above.

1 Work out the population density for Egypt.

2 Describe the distribution of the Egyptian population (how it is spread out).

3 Why is the population density figure misleading?

4 Give two reasons why area A would be unsuitable for large numbers of people.

5 Give two reasons why area B is suitable for inhabitation.

BIRTH AND DEATH RATES AND POPULATION SIZE

By comparing birth rates and death rates for a particular country we can work out whether the population is rising or falling. If the birth rate is higher than the death rate then the population will rise. The greater the difference, the greater the rate of natural increase. The rate of natural increase is much higher in developing countries of the world.

ACTION!

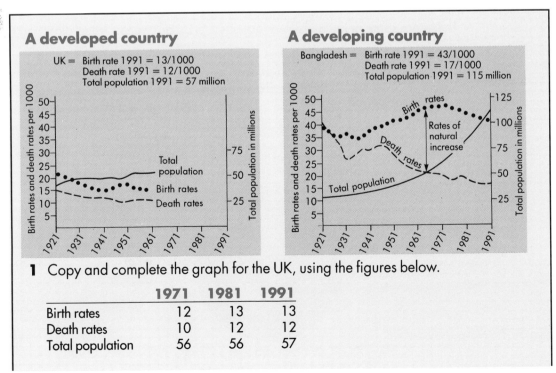

1 Copy and complete the graph for the UK, using the figures below.

	1971	1981	1991
Birth rates	12	13	13
Death rates	10	12	12
Total population	56	56	57

2 Shade the area of the graph showing the 'natural increase'.

3 Look at the graph for Bangladesh.
(a) In which year were death rates higher than birth rates?
(b) What would happen to the total population during this time?

4 Compare the two graphs. Identify four differences and two similarities between the two countries.

POPULATION CHANGE

The world's population is growing very rapidly and for the past 100 years or so the Earth has experienced a **population explosion**.

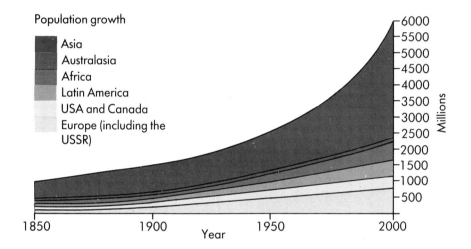

Knowing what the total population will be in a few years time is very important. The following points must be carefully estimated:

How many houses will be needed?
How much food will have to be grown?
What about the number of schools?

These are some of the questions that need to be answered when planning for the future.

Not everywhere in the world has had the same rate of change. The most rapid growth in population has occurred in the poorer, developing countries while the richer, developed countries have seen little or no growth. Also, in many countries, millions of people have moved from the countryside into urban areas. As a result of this, the latter part of the century has seen a rapid increase in the number of people living in cities.

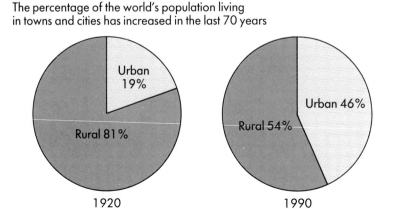

The percentage of the world's population living in towns and cities has increased in the last 70 years

120

The total population will change when the balance between the number of people being born (the birth rate) and the number of people who die (the death rate) changes. The number of people moving into or out of an area (migration) also influences population change.

ACTION!

Complete the 'population change' column in the table below by putting the following phrases in the correct place:
Little change   Rapid increase   Rapid decrease

Birth rate	Death rate	Migration	Population change	Example
Few being born	Few die	Few move in or out		A developed country such as the UK
Many being born	Few die	Few move in or out	Rapid increase	A developing country such as Kenya
Many being born	Many die	Many moving in		A city in the developing world
Few being born	Few die	Many moving out		Rural areas of Britain

ACTION!

People's attitudes to family size is one of the factors that controls the birth rate. Again, we can compare the opinions of a typical family from the developed world with one from a developing country.

Study the cartoons above.

1 Suggest two reasons why families in developed countries generally have fewer children.

2 Why are children so important to parents in developing countries? Suggest two reasons.

3 What do the cartoons suggest about the standard of health care in the two countries?

WHY PEOPLE MOVE

The total number of people moving into or out of an area can also affect the size of the population. **Migration** can take place within a country or between two countries; over long distances or short distances; it can be temporary (for a short period of time) or permanent.

A **migrant** is the term used to describe someone who moves from place to place. An **immigrant** is someone who moves into an area and an **emigrant** is someone who moves out. Some people may move because they want to, while others may be forced out of their homes.

ACTION!

Below are listed some of the reasons why people move. Copy the table, putting each reason in the correct column.

Reasons
wanting a new house   marriage
fear of persecution   retirement
nearer to friends and relatives
disease   famine   war
chance of job promotion
attractive area

A forced move	A move through choice

Case study: The Ernie Martin story

Ernie was born in India. During his life he has moved home on no less than eight occasions.

Year	From	To	Reason	Advantages
1962	India	Brighton, England	Whole family, including mother, father, two brothers and two sisters came to England	Make new friends and watch test cricket
1964	Brighton	Haywards Heath	Nurse's training	Opportunity for independence
1969	Haywards Heath	Edinburgh	Further training	Increases skills, so increases job opportunities
1972	Edinburgh	London	Advance in career	Closer to family in Brighton
1975	London	Brighton	Family reason	Family needed support
1975	Brighton	London	Career prospects	More responsible job
1979	London	Stafford	Aim to settle down with wife	Change of career focus. Now a job with a high profile
1988	Stafford	Boston, Lincolnshire	Promotion	Positive change of lifestyle; better for the family

ACTION!

1 In an atlas, find a map of Britain. Try to locate each of the British towns Ernie has lived in.

2 How many times did Ernie move for (a) his career; (b) his family?

3 Do you think he likes living in Boston? Why?

Case study: Kurdish migration

In the early part of 1991 most of the Kurdish nation was 'on the move'. They were forced out from their homes because they felt their safety was being threatened by civil war.

Kurdistan had become part of the larger country of Iraq in 1922, but the Kurds never accepted themselves as Iraqis — they were Kurds first! Lack of co-operation between the Kurds and the Iraqi government has led to constant disagreement and occasional fighting.

At the end of the Gulf War the Iraqi government decided to launch attacks against the Kurds. Many Kurds felt this was the last straw and the only option they had was to abandon their land and homes and flee across the mountains to Iran and Turkey.

Kurds on the move

In many cases Turkey felt that they could not cope with the millions of migrants flooding across the border. They simply did not have enough food or resources. The Kurds were grouped together in huge 'camps' on the mountainside with little food, no water and no sanitation. They just had to wait for politicians to decide their fate.

Fresh water is rare on such a move

'Please don't send us back' beg refugees

Kurdish refugees yesterday pleaded with Foreign Office Minister Linda Chalker to save them from Saddam Hussein's clutches.

Everyone she spoke to in the sprawling border camp at Isikveren, Turkey, told her they did not want to go back to Iraq – even if they are protected by Allied troops.

Mothers held out their emaciated and filthy children as they begged Mrs Chalker for help, but one old man in traditional guerrilla gear shook her hand and said: 'Thank you Britain, thank you'.

Another grabbed her arm and said 'We can never go back while Saddam is still there. The best thing we want is to remove Saddam.'

Patiently, Mrs Chalker told him: 'We understand that, but we must get you warm food and clothes and keep you strong.'

ACTION!

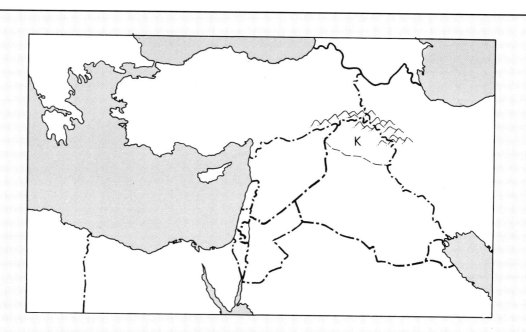

1 Use an atlas to find the eleven countries shown on the map.

2 The area marked 'K' is where most of the Kurds live. Draw two arrows showing the direction of movement.

3 Why do you think the Kurds were forced to move?

4 List three problems they have faced on their journey.

5 Why do you think that the Kurds don't want to go back, as suggested by the newspaper article?

UNIT 12
Where people live

THE LOCATION OF SETTLEMENTS

The places where people live are called **settlements**. There are different types of settlements which have grown for different reasons. They may be small villages with houses and a few shops, or large towns with many houses, shopping centres, offices and factories.

Often, by looking at the history of an area, we can find out why some settlements began. An important clue is in the name of the settlement. The table gives some examples.

Origin of placename	Part of the placename	Meaning
Celts Originally from South Germany 2500 – 0 BC	Aber Inver Tre - Pen - Llan - Pont -	Mouth of Town Top of a hill Church Bridge
Romans Originally from Italy 0 – 400 AD	-caster -chester -cester	Fort or castle
Saxons Originally from North Germany 400 – 600 AD	-borough -bury -ing -am -ton -wich	Fort Group of people Homestead Enclosure Market
Vikings From Norway and Denmark 600 – 1000 AD	-by -ey -dale -thorpe -ford	Enclosure Island Valley Smaller village River crossing

We call the place where a settlement is built the **site**. Again, history can give us a clue as to why settlements grew where they did. Some examples include:

Early sites were often chosen because they were easy to defend against attacks from enemies. **Defensive** sites are often found on hills or in the loop of a river bend.

Rivers could only be crossed at certain places where it was possible to build a bridge. A **bridging point** was a good site for a settlement.

Some settlements grew next to streams or springs – water was just as essential in those days. These are **wet point** sites.

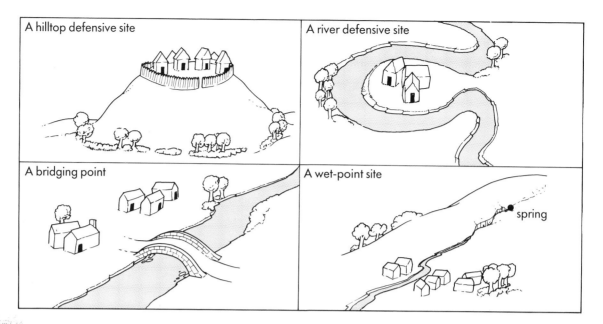

A hilltop defensive site

A river defensive site

A bridging point

A wet-point site

spring

ACTION!

1   In an atlas find a map of Britain. Using the place name table, list examples of four Celtic settlements, four Roman, four Saxon and four Viking settlements.

2

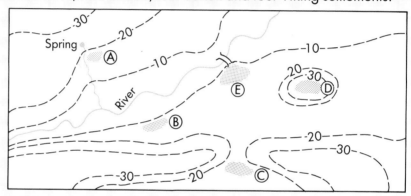

Spring

River

The map above shows five settlements (indicated by letters) whose **site** has been influenced by the landscape. Match the reasons for setting up with the letters:

Dry point settlement (away from flood risk) _____

Gap town (between two hills) _____

Defensive site _____

Wet point settlement _____

Bridging point _____

3   Copy the diagram above.
Shade in blue the area of the map most likely to be flooded.
Join each of the towns with a main road.

Which town is most likely to grow into the largest settlement? _____

Why? _____

_____

Which settlement is likely to have a castle? _____

Why? _____

_____

SETTLEMENT PATTERNS: THE SHAPE OF TOWNS

The shape all the buildings in a town make is called a **settlement pattern**. The pattern of a settlement is usually affected by the slope of the land around it.

A dispersed pattern (spread out)

This sort of settlement is found in areas where the people need a lot of land, such as in farming areas, or if the land is hilly so that only a few buildings can be built.

A linear pattern (straight line)

This sort of settlement is found in a valley where the steep valley sides prevent growth of the town. Linear settlements may also be found along roads.

A nucleated pattern (close together)

This pattern is found where buildings in a town are built around a central point. This pattern is often found on flat, lowland areas, when in the past, houses were built close to each other for protection.

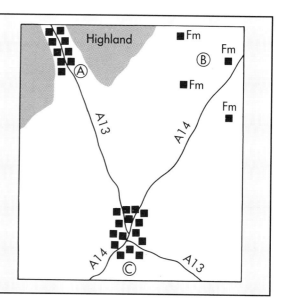

1 Which of the settlements labelled A, B and C on the sketch map is: nucleated   dispersed   linear?

2 What is the central point of settlement C?

3 Give one reason why settlement A has developed in this way.

4 What is the most likely occupation of the owners of the houses in settlement B?

FUNCTIONS OF TOWNS

When a settlement is begun there has to be a reason for that settlement to grow. This reason is called a **function**. The function is the main purpose of a settlement. There are different types of functions. Here are some examples:

1 Market town
Most market towns began when much of the population were farmers who needed somewhere to sell their produce and where they could also buy things they needed, such as tools, seeds and anvils.

A market town

An administration centre

2 Administration centre
The function of this settlement is to deal with all the work involved in running a large area, such as a county. There are many offices here such as the County Hall, police headquarters and law courts.

3 Holiday resort
This is a place people visit for holidays. The main function of a resort is to provide a place where people can enjoy themselves and relax.

4 Port
A port is a place where goods can be brought into the country or sent to other countries by ship. Goods which are brought into a port are called **imports** while goods sent out from a port are called **exports**.

A resort

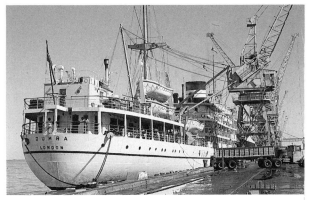
A port

5 Industrial centre

The main function of this type of settlement is the production of goods in factories. Other industrial towns may be based around a coal mine. These settlements are usually not as old as market towns.

An industrial centre

ACTION!

1 Match the correct letter shown on the map with the correct function listed below:

port   administration centre   resort   market centre   industry

2 There are three industrial towns. Which ones would contain:

(a) Coal mine _____

(b) Glass works _____

(c) Brick works _____

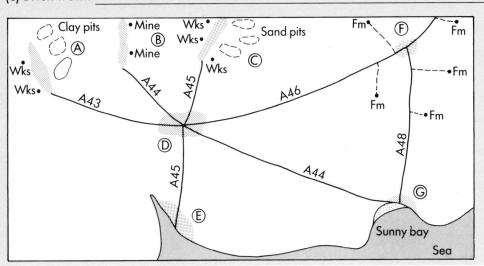

3 Which town is likely to contain the only sports centre of the area?

Town _____

Why? _____

4 Where would you locate a fun fair?

Town _____

Why? _____

5 Which town is likely to contain a centre for agricultural machinery?

Town _____

Why? _____

6 Tesco plans to build a large superstore in the area. Near which town do you think would be the best location? _____

Why? _____

SETTLEMENT HIERARCHY: WHERE TO SHOP?

Some settlements are more important than others because of their functions. A settlement hierarchy is a way of putting settlements into order of importance.

The main way of deciding which settlements are more important is to look at the goods and services provided. Some goods and services are needed every day – these are called **low order** e.g. groceries, newspapers. Other goods and services are needed less frequently, perhaps once or twice a month, such as banks, clothing – these are **middle order** goods and services. **High order** goods and services are required less often, perhaps only once or twice a year or less, such as jewellers, opticians, furniture, electrical goods. Usually, most people are prepared to travel further, or make a special journey to obtain **high order goods** The settlements that provide these goods and functions can be classified in the same way.

A hierarchy can be shown in a diagram

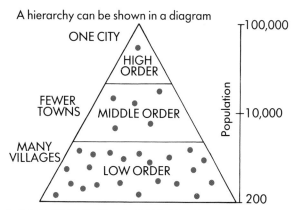

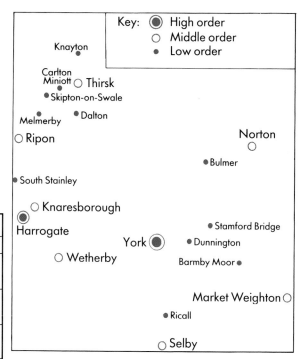

Settlement	Goods and services provided	Order
Hamlet	Small shop, maybe no services at all.	Low
Village	Small shop, post office, church. Maybe small primary school.	Low
Small town	Several shops, supermarkets, banks, doctors, dentist.	Middle
Large town	Shopping centre, several supermarkets. Jewellers, clothing and shoe shops.	Middle
City	Electrical goods, solicitors, shopping complexes, large hospital, cinemas, theatres.	High

ACTION!

HOW SMALL SETTLEMENTS CHANGE THROUGH TIME

Case study: Minehead

The town of Minehead is situated on the edge of the Exmoor National Park. Its origins date back to the eleventh century when it was an agricultural settlement but it became more important as a port during the sixteenth century. A fire in 1791 destroyed the centre of Minehead, which was then rebuilt and as the port declined the tourist trade grew with the attraction of nearby Exmoor. Today Minehead is a family resort with the added attraction of 'Somerwest World', formerly a Butlin's holiday camp, which can cater for up to 10 000 people – doubling the population of Minehead in the summer.

But Minehead is changing

There are currently plans to restructure part of the sea front with houses, flats and holiday apartments. The proposed site is a disused lido and the surrounding land. Almost 300 new dwellings are planned.

Local people are divided in their opinion of the development. Some people think that the town needs more high quality housing. Others believe that the land could be better used for recreational facilities for the town because those at Somerwest World are too expensive for the locals.

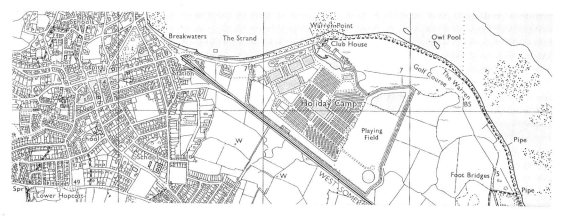

ACTION!

£16m Seafront Housing Plan

Details of a £16 million proposal to restructure Minehead's eastern seafront with houses, flats, luxury holiday apartments and a sheltered housing scheme, putting Minehead among the forefront of Britain's seaside resorts, was revealed by the Rank Organisation this week.

As the giant holiday company ended months of speculation, town and district councillors welcomed the investment in a holiday town which has been hamstrung this year by the dilapidated condition of the seafront lido site and the 'road to nowhere' status of the new seafront relief road which stopped short at the Somerwest World holiday centre.

Now all the wrangling is over and on Wednesday George Rushton, of Rank holiday and leisure division, announced: 'I am pleased to say that we have reached agreement with county and district councils over the road and we will not only be dedicating the land but also will make a significant contribution towards the cost of constructing and completing the road.'

The sum of £165 000 has been speculated as the probable contribution by Rank, but Mr Rushton would not commit himself to a figure. He said construction should be completed over the winter of 1990/91.

He made it plain that this agreement for the completion of the road depends upon district planners giving the go-ahead to Rank's plans for developing the 11-acre lido site, which has lain derelict since they acquired it 5 years ago, and 2 adjoining acres now occupied by the Arnold Palmer Leisure Centre, which at present provides such amusements as crazy golf and go-karting.

It is unlikely that Rank will encounter any planning difficulties, but district planning officer Colin Russell said such a comprehensive scheme would need careful investigation and it would be some three months before a decision could be finalised.

The plan for providing almost 300 new dwellings includes 36 terraced or semi-detached houses, 80 luxury seafront flats and 102 sheltered homes, all for sale.

From: The Somerset County Gazette, 24 November 1989

Read the article above and use your own knowledge to answer the following questions:

1 (a) What are the advantages for local people of the planned redevelopment?
   (b) Are there any disadvantages?

2 Do you think it will help the tourist trade? If so, how?

URBAN ZONES: DIFFERENT AREAS WITHIN TOWNS

As towns have grown in size their original reason for being at a particular site has been lost. Development brings with it different functions. Large towns and cities that have grown from first settlements now have more than one function – usually shops and offices (**commerce**), housing (**residential**), factories (**industry**) and parks and playing fields (**recreation**).

You may have noticed when travelling through different towns that they resemble each other in the way they are laid out. For example, the main shopping areas are found in the centre; the style and age of the housing seems to get more modern as you move towards the edges of the town and any industries are usually found together. If we look closely at the layout of towns it is possible to identify areas or **zones**. The diagram overleaf shows an example of a model town. Each ring shows a zone.

Zone 1

The town centre or CBD (**central business district**). Many shops, banks and restaurants are found here. The bus station and train station are found here. Many different businesses would like to locate here. Land is expensive, so buildings are tall with several floors. Few houses.

Zone 2

This area of the town was built in the last century. Then, it would have been full of factories and small terraced houses for the workers. Today this area is called the inner city. Many of the factories have been demolished, modernised or replaced.

Greenbelt

Greenbelt

1 2 3 4

Zone 3

This zone is nearly all residential. The large houses would have been built in the 1920s and 1930s. We call this area the inner suburbs.

Zone 4

This is the newest part of the town. Here there are modern housing estates and some council estates. You will also find small, modern factories here and some large 'out-of-town' superstores. There are more parks and open spaces. Land is cheaper.

In order to prevent towns and cities from growing too large and taking up even more land a law was passed which enabled town and city councils to set up a **green belt** around the town. This meant that building and development is strictly controlled in the green belt. This has been successful in some cases in stopping too much growth, but in other places developers have built on the land beyond the green belt, so that the green belt is almost another zone of the town.

ACTION!

Field work/enquiry

Make a journey from the edge of your nearest town into the town centre. Things to look for:

- Are there any changes in the age of the houses?
- Do you notice any changes in the size of the houses?
- Do you pass any factories – what are they like, old or new?
- Does the amount of open space change as you move into the town centre?
- Where do the houses stop and offices and shops start?
- Are there any buildings that have more than one storey – if so, where?

1 Try to draw a diagram of your journey into town.

2 Locate the CBD and see if you can identify the zones labelled in the model.

3 Does your town fit this model?

URBAN DEVELOPMENT

Towns and cities do not stay the same as time passes. Some parts are modernised and renewed while others fall into disrepair and decay. What causes areas in a town to change?

- Town centres are popular areas for business, so need to be modernised to attract people.
- Industry may move to bigger or more modern factories.
- Older, terraced houses are small and need more money spent on them to keep them in good repair.
- Sometimes whole sections of towns can fall into disrepair because the original function has declined.

The renewal or modernisation of towns and cities is called **redevelopment.** An example of large-scale redevelopment is taking place in the dockland areas of London and Cardiff. As the importance of the docks declined large areas of these cities were left derelict. Modernisation has created new offices, modern industrial units and luxury apartment blocks.

Case study: Cardiff Bay redevelopment

History

In 1890 Cardiff was a thriving port. It exported coal from South Wales all over the world. Since then its importance has gradually declined until by the 1950s and 1960s large areas of former docklands had become derelict. In the 1980s a 10-year development plan was proposed to regenerate the Cardiff Bay area. The scheme is now awaiting the final go-ahead from Parliament. Permission to start will only be given if a number of problems can be overcome.

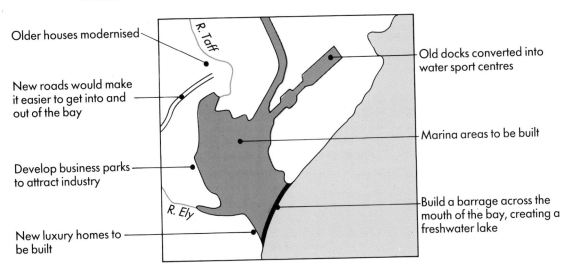

Older houses modernised

New roads would make it easier to get into and out of the bay

Develop business parks to attract industry

New luxury homes to be built

R. Taff

R. Ely

Old docks converted into water sport centres

Marina areas to be built

Build a barrage across the mouth of the bay, creating a freshwater lake

Problems to be overcome

– Local houses may be prone to flooding as groundwater may rise into their cellars.

– Sewage coming down the River Taff may not be allowed out to sea.

– Large areas of mudflats will be destroyed so birds will not be able to feed.

– House prices may shoot up so local people will not be able to afford them.

ACTION!

Emily lives with her mum, dad and two sisters in an area of Cardiff likely to be affected by the Cardiff Bay redevelopment. Like most of her neighbourhood Emily is against the scheme. Her dad holds a different view.

Emily says:

– Local communities will break up due to all the newcomers buying expensive houses

– It may cause flooding

– There is no reason to destroy the wildlife areas

– Development should go on in peaceful ways and not be imposed upon people

– The quality of water in the river may deteriorate

Her father says:

– At present at low tide it looks awful. If the scheme goes ahead it will be more pleasing to the eye

– It needs drastic action to clean the river. If they build the barrage the river will have to be kept clean

– Lower Cardiff needs to be developed as growth may go to other areas, destroying other environments and leading to the growth of towns

– Many people are against it because they are concerned about the value of their property

1 Read Emily's comments on the previous page. List three things that concern her about the barrage.

2 List three benefits Emily's father thinks the building of the barrage will bring to Cardiff.

3 If you lived in Cardiff would you be for or against the scheme? Give reasons for your answer.

Artist's impression of the Cardiff Bay barrage

UNIT 13
Transport

THE IMPORTANCE OF TRANSPORT

Transport is very important in the modern world. Much of our daily lives is governed by how and why people and goods move from place to place. **Goods** are everyday items that people and industry need – for example, food, fuels, metals and washing machines. When people are transported they are called **passengers** and when goods are transported they are called **freight.**

There are many different forms of transport. The type of transport you would choose to use depends on a number of factors:

- How far are you travelling?
- How long will it take you to get there?
- What will you be carrying?
- How much will it cost?
- How often do you make that particular journey?

METHODS OF TRANSPORT

For goods						
	Overland				**Sea**	**Air**
	Van	**Lorry**	**Rail**	**Pipeline**	**Ship**	**Aircraft**
Used for	small items e.g. local items	light goods + foodstuffs	Large bulky goods e.g. iron ore	Fuels e.g. gas + oil	Large heavy bulky goods e.g. coal	small expensive goods e.g. flowers
Cost	quite cheap	quite cheap	quite expensive	very cheap	cheap	very expensive
Advantages	flexible	flexible	large quantities quickly transported	direct	large quantities transported	very quick
Disadvantages	slow + congestion	slow + pollution	better links with major cities only	only 2 places linked	very slow	only places near airports can be served

For passengers					
	Overland			**Sea**	**Air**
	car	**coach**	**rail**	**ferry**	**air**
No. of passengers	5	50+	100+	500+	300+
Cost	cheap	cheap	quite expensive	quite cheap	very expensive
Advantages	can choose when to travel	regular service	direct routes	used as a link across the sea	speed
Disadvantages	congested roads	slow	only major towns served	slow	cost

Listed below is a series of journeys. List the most appropriate type or types of transport used in each case.

- A touring holiday in France.
- Visiting friends at their house across town.
- Oil from the North Sea to the British mainland.
- An important parcel for Australia.
- A business meeting in Rome.
- Visiting an aunt 250 miles away.

DIFFERENT ROUTES

A straight line between two places is the shortest distance, so that is normally the quickest and cheapest **route** to take. But it is not always the easiest. It may not be possible to choose the most **direct** route. **Detours** may sometimes have to be made.

When roads and railways are being built, engineers and planners have to take many things into account.

Different ways of getting from main town to main port

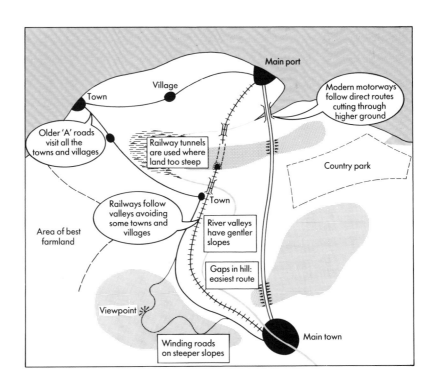

139

Linking places

The roads and railways that link places together make up a **network**. If there are many roads and railways then the network is well developed – places would be **accessible**, i.e. easy to get to. Few roads and railways in an area means that the network is poorly developed so places would be difficult to get to, i.e. **inaccessible**. A transport network gives us an indication of how easy it is for goods and people to move from place to place.

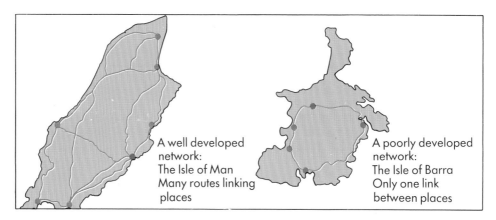

A well developed network:
The Isle of Man
Many routes linking places

A poorly developed network:
The Isle of Barra
Only one link between places

ACTION!

You have been given the task of building a railway line linking three towns – A, B and C. The aim is to find the cheapest possible route. When you have found the cheapest route, draw your railway line on the map and write the total cost below.

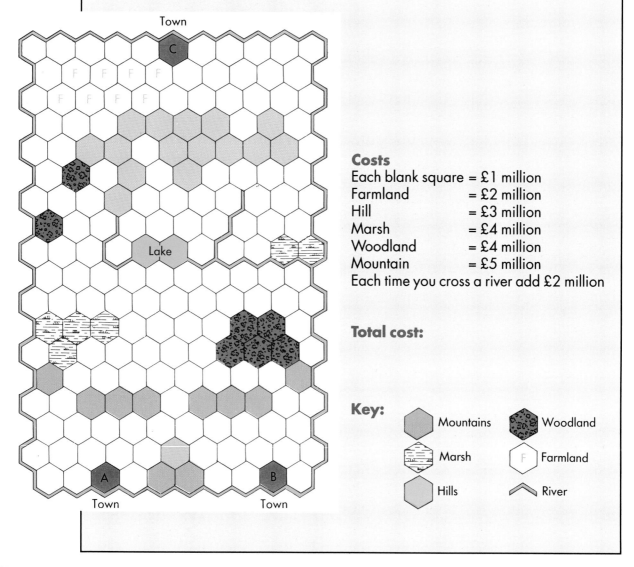

Costs
Each blank square = £1 million
Farmland   = £2 million
Hill   = £3 million
Marsh   = £4 million
Woodland   = £4 million
Mountain   = £5 million
Each time you cross a river add £2 million

Total cost:

Key:

Mountains   Woodland
Marsh   Farmland
Hills   River

TOO MUCH TRAFFIC!

Traffic jams are common in many towns and cities. Nowadays there are so many cars, buses, vans and lorries trying to use the roads that traffic congestion in towns is a frequent occurrence. The problems are particularly bad during 'rush hours' – the times when many people are travelling to and from work. Too much traffic can lead to a number of problems:

- Pollution from exhaust fumes can be a health risk, as well as causing damage to buildings.
- Traffic is very noisy and can cause windows to shake.
- People caught in the traffic jams waste time, which may cost businesses money and can be frustrating for drivers.
- Heavy traffic can lead to an increase in accidents.

Reasons for increase in traffic:

- Older houses do not have garages, so cars are parked on the streets.
- Nowadays people own more cars.
- Many businesses prefer to use road transport rather than rail.
- There has been a large increase in the number of company cars.
- The number of lorries using the roads has also increased.
- People prefer to travel by car, as public transport can be slow, unreliable and expensive.
- Town centres were built before cars were invented, so streets are often narrow, with many road junctions.
- Road works and repairs can disrupt normal traffic flows.

ACTION!

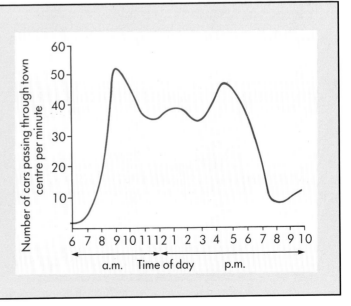

1 (a) Conduct a survey in your class. How many of your class ride in a car at least once a day?

(b) How many use public transport at least once a day?

2 Look at the line graph opposite, which shows traffic flow in a town centre.

Describe and account for the pattern shown by the graph.

Are there solutions to the problem?

There are basically two ways of reducing the amount of traffic using town centres.

Either:

Introduce traffic management schemes which would enable traffic to move more easily through or around the town centre.

Problems

- Schemes like this are usually expensive.
- They use up more valuable land in the town centre.
- They encourage people to use their cars even more.

A one-way system

Or:

Make it very difficult and expensive for traffic to move around and through the town so that people will be encouraged to leave their cars at home.

Problem

- People are so used to the convenience of cars that they would probably take a lot of persuasion to change their attitudes.

A way of slowing down traffic: 'sleeping policemen' on a road in Cardiff

ACTION!

Copy into the table below each of the schemes under the correct heading:

Would lead to **more** cars being used	Would lead to **less** cars being used

1 Introduce one-way systems:

2 Make public transport more reliable, comfortable and frequent.

3 Build a multi-storey car park in the town centre.

4 Increase the price of petrol and make fares on public transport very cheap.

5 Build a by-pass around the town.

6 Restrict movement in town centres by pedestrianising shopping areas.

7 Give priority to buses and bicycles in town centres.

8 Build a series of roundabouts at problem junctions.

9 Cut down on the number of car parking spaces and increase charges.

10 Introduce traffic lights.

Where to build a by-pass?

Sometimes a by-pass may be the only solution to a particular traffic problem. Take Little Dollington, for example. Little Dollington is a village with a busy main road running straight through the middle of it. The road is used by hundreds of lorries every day, going to and coming from the local quarry.

Why is a by-pass needed?

'My children's school is right on the main road. They have to cross it at the busiest times of day. I'm worried that there will be a serious accident one day.' (A young mother)

'I have to drive through Little Dollington every day. It adds at least 20 minutes onto my journey and I only have to go a few miles. I use lots of fuel and spend most of my time stuck in a traffic jam.' (A lorry driver)

'My shop is in the High Street. There is so much dirt from the traffic that I can't display my produce outside. My delivery lorries have trouble unloading and customers won't cross the busy road.' (A greengrocer)

'I live on the main road. Every time a lorry goes past my windows rattle! I can't hang washing out – it comes off the line dirty. In the summer I can't open my windows because of the fumes and noise'. (A local resident)

But where do we build the by-pass?

Choosing a route for a by-pass is never easy. There are many things that have to be taken into account.

ACTION!

1 Look at the sketch map below which shows three possible by-pass routes round Little Dollington. Each one has its problems. Describe the problems associated with each of the routes.

2 The by-pass will cost a quarter of a million pounds for every kilometre. Which route will be the cheapest?

3 Which route do you think should be chosen and why?

A by-pass route for Little Dollington: but which one?

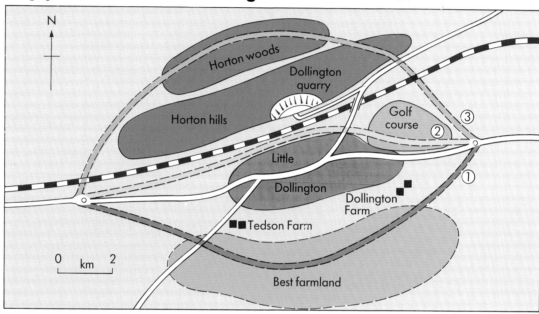

HOW TRANSPORT CHANGES WITH CHANGES IN TECHNOLOGY

Case study: Getting across the Channel

At present
How? Ferry, hovercraft
Why? To move freight and people

Calais car ferry terminal, France

Advantages
– Variety of routes
– Cheaper than building a fixed link
– Chance for restful break in journey
– Employment for crews and at ports
– Can be fairly quick, for shorter routes

Disadvantages
– Time regarding length of journey
– Limited number of crossings due to tides
– Limited amount of freight/traffic can be carried
– Weather can cause delays

In future
How? The Channel Tunnel
Why? To move more freight and more people
　　　　Increase in traffic
　　　　Technology available

Advantages
– Quicker, so cuts costs
– Crossings not dependent on weather
– Less congestion at Channel ports
– Fewer lorries on road, so less pollution
– Direct link to Europe – more trade
– No danger to shipping

How the main terminal will look

Disadvantages
– High cost of construction
– Environmental damage, e.g. building terminals, disposing of waste from tunnel
– Encourages road traffic in a small area
– Links for terminal use land
– Safety – animals could bring rabies through tunnel
– Easier for drug smugglers and terrorists to operate
– Job losses in ferry companies

How the tunnel works

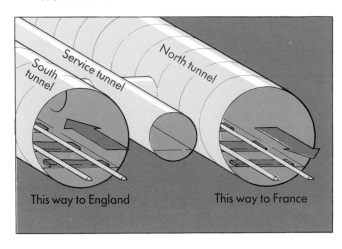

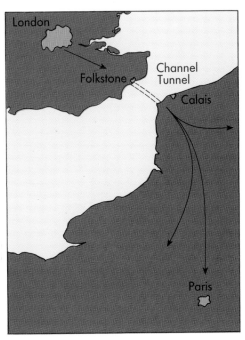

- The tunnel is about 50km long, from Ashford in Kent to Fréthun near Calais.
- Two separate tunnels (one north and one south) are linked by a service tunnel to carry a rail line.
- Travel through the tunnel is on special shuttle trains which will leave every 10–15 minutes. The journey takes about 35 minutes from terminal to terminal.
- The next step is to have a high-speed link between London and Paris on a special train so there can be travel straight through.

For all parts of Britain to benefit, direct links are needed from other major cities in England, Scotland and Wales. Also freight lines, with direct routes to the Tunnel, would need to be built, then new industry could be attracted.

ACTION!

1 From the list of people below, choose who would be for the building of the tunnel and who would be against.

- A steward on a cross-Channel ferry.
- A building worker living in Folkestone.
- A farmer in south-east England, through whose land the motorway link runs.
- An Edinburgh-based businessman.
- English people with holiday homes in northern France.
- A customs officer with responsibility for controlling rabies.
- A villager who lives near Folkestone.
- A chairwoman of an international business firm living in Paris.

2 If you lived in Kent would you be for or against the building of the tunnel? State why.

UNIT 14
Using the land

COMPETITION FOR LAND

Land is used in many different ways:

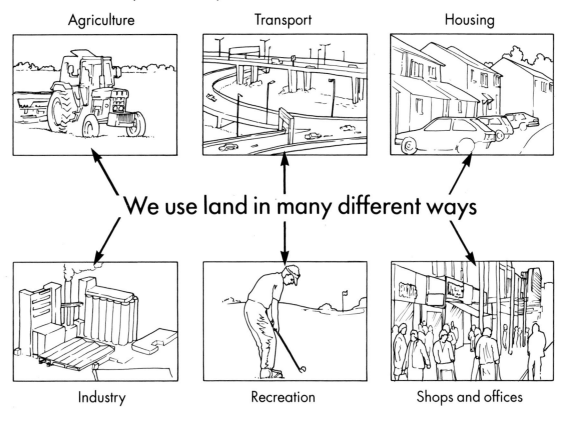

Agriculture   Transport   Housing

We use land in many different ways

Industry   Recreation   Shops and offices

Some activities require a large amount of land, while others need only a small area. If a piece of land is in a desirable location, several companies may compete to own it. If there are many people interested in buying a piece of land, it becomes more valuable and its price goes up.

ACTION!

1 Do the following activities require large or small areas of land?
a golf course   a farm   a sports centre   a shoe shop
an industrial complex   a house   a three-lane motorway   an airport

2 Which two of the following phrases, if true, would lead to an increase in land values (the other two would lead to a decrease)?

Barratts building a housing estate on poor quality farmland

The local council giving permission for a waste disposal site nearby

Breaching of a sea wall, increasing the risk of flooding

Building a link road, increasing accessibility

HOW FARMLAND IS USED

Farmland can be used in a variety of ways:

| *Arable* Farmers grow crops such as wheat or barley | *Pastoral* Farmers look after animals such as dairy cows or sheep | *Mixed* Farming involves crops and animals | Farming can be done in large buildings such as greenhouses, chicken houses or stalls |

The soil is possibly the earth's most valuable resource. Without it, plants would not grow, so farmers would not be able to grow our food. In fact there would be very little life on earth.

Many of today's farmers are destroying that resource. All over the world large areas of land have become useless for agriculture because the soil has been washed away by rainwater or blown away by the wind – this is soil erosion, and is the result of modern farming methods.

The causes of soil erosion

Deforestation (cutting down trees) means raindrops hit the soil directly. Also, there are no roots to bind the soil together.

Fields are left bare during autumn, when storms are common. Heavy rain can lead to soil being washed away and deep gullies forming.

oughing straight p and down ills means soil washed away down e furrows.

More run-off means more water in the river, which can lead to extra erosion of the river banks.

eavy machinery ompacts the soil nd erosion occurs own tractor heelings.

Monoculture (growing the same crop in a field year after year) results in the same nutrients being taken out. The soil can become crumbly and can easily blow away.

praying and rtilising fields ruins e structure of the oil, causing it to reak up. It is then asily blown away y the wind.

Too many animals in a field leads to overgrazing and loss of vegetation. This is particularly a problem in poorer, drier countries.

ACTION!

Can the rate of soil erosion be reduced?

Look at all the information in the illustration above.

Match the numbered 'solutions' to soil erosion with the correct lettered 'problem that would be solved', e.g. solution 1 should be matched with problem E.

Solutions

1 Plant hedgerows as boundaries for smaller fields.

2 Contour ploughing – ploughing across the slope.

3 Introduce crop rotation – not growing the same crop in a field every year.

4 Plant trees to act as wind breaks.

5 Use more organic fertilisers and farm in an organic way.

6 Control the number of animals allowed to graze in a particular field.

Problem that would be solved

A Fields would be sheltered from the wind, so the soil would not be blown away.

B Reduces the risk of overgrazing.

C Balance the nutrients taken out of and returned to the soil.

D Stop rainwater running down furrows, washing soil away.

E Roots of hedges would bind the soil together.

F Artificial fertilisers wil not damage the soil structure.

Case study: Coed Morgan Farm

Coed Morgan Farm is a dairy farm in south-east Wales. Mr Meadmore, the farmer, also grows some cereal crops (known as fodder crops) which he feeds to his animals in winter. He also keeps some beef cattle and some sheep.

Some farming terms

Permanent pasture Fields that are always grass and used as pasture land for animals.

Silage Grass that is cut green and kept to feed animals in winter.

Ley grass Grass that is planted. Fields with ley grass are occasionally ploughed up.

Crop rotation Different crops grown in each field every year, as part of a cycle.

Facts and figures

Number of hectares	74
Workers – Full-time	2
– Part-time	1
Dairy cows	62
Beef cattle	107
Sheep	200
Lambs	200

The farmer's income

Milk	50%	Beef	32%
Cereals	10%	Sheep	8%

10-year crop rotation cycle

The crops grown in the same field over a ten-year period

Year	1	2	3	4	5	6	7	8	9	10
Crop	Wheat	Maize	Oats	Wheat	Barley	Ley grass	→			

How Mr Meadmore uses his land

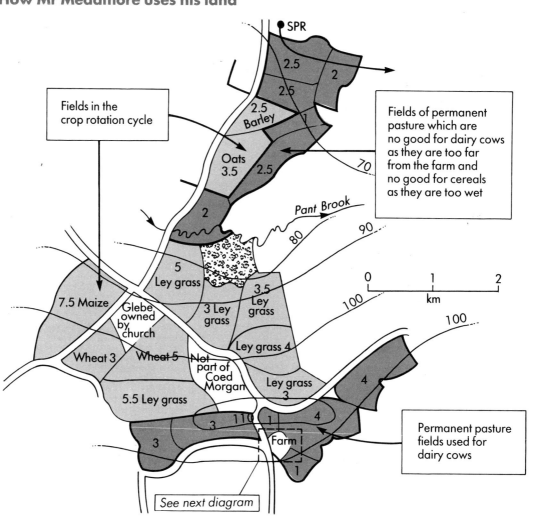

Fields in the crop rotation cycle

Fields of permanent pasture which are no good for dairy cows as they are too far from the farm and no good for cereals as they are too wet

Permanent pasture fields used for dairy cows

See next diagram

150

Plan of Coed Morgan Farm buildings

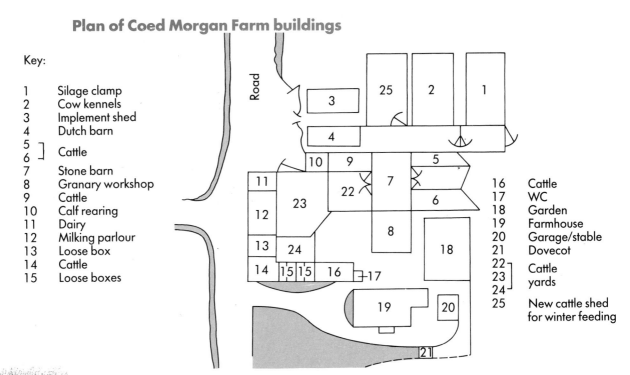

Key:

1 Silage clamp
2 Cow kennels
3 Implement shed
4 Dutch barn
5
6] Cattle
7 Stone barn
8 Granary workshop
9 Cattle
10 Calf rearing
11 Dairy
12 Milking parlour
13 Loose box
14 Cattle
15 Loose boxes

16 Cattle
17 WC
18 Garden
19 Farmhouse
20 Garage/stable
21 Dovecot
22
23] Cattle yards
24
25 New cattle shed for winter feeding

ACTION!

1 Name four dairy products.

2 The fields furthest from the farm are not suitable for dairy cows. Why do you think this is so?

3 (a) What is crop rotation?
(b) Why does the farmer grow grass for five years in succession?

4 Use the table labelled 'farmer's income' to draw a pie graph.
Hints: pie graphs are useful to show percentages. They are circles.
Each circle/graph is 360° all round, so if we want to check a portion of the circle, we need to use a simple calculation.
Every 1% = 3.6°, so for example 10% = 10 x 3.6 = 36°.

HOW INDUSTRY USES LAND

A large proportion of land in Britain is given over to industry. Some industries require large areas of land, while others need only enough land on which to build a small factory. Industrial complexes such as the ICI plant on Teesside cover several square miles. Smaller factories are mainly grouped together on industrial estates or in business parks.

A steelworks

An industrial estate

151

The advantages of locating similar activities together

Lots of factories are usually found together on a Trading Estate. They are not there by accident. Each factory takes advantage of a particular set of circumstances – see diagram below.

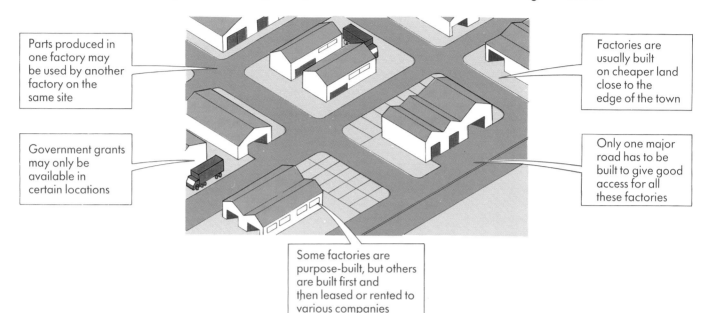

Parts produced in one factory may be used by another factory on the same site

Government grants may only be available in certain locations

Factories are usually built on cheaper land close to the edge of the town

Only one major road has to be built to give good access for all these factories

Some factories are purpose-built, but others are built first and then leased or rented to various companies

Case study: Shoe shops

In any High Street, shoe shops can often be found next door to each other. The reason is that shoes are an example of **middle cost goods**. People don't buy shoes every day, so they would be prepared to make a special journey to buy them. They are also **comparison** goods. People will compare prices and styles before deciding on which pair to buy. It is therefore an advantage to have such shops together – people don't want to walk long distances between shops.

ACTION!

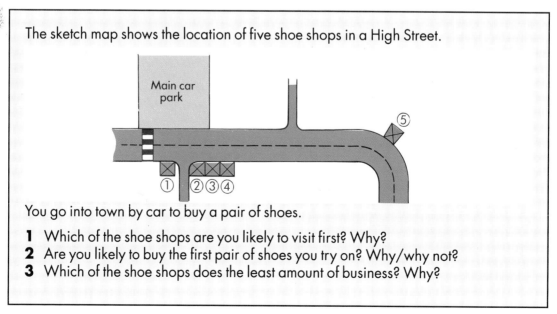

The sketch map shows the location of five shoe shops in a High Street.

You go into town by car to buy a pair of shoes.

1 Which of the shoe shops are you likely to visit first? Why?
2 Are you likely to buy the first pair of shoes you try on? Why/why not?
3 Which of the shoe shops does the least amount of business? Why?

HOW SUPERSTORES USE LAND

A plan view of a typical store

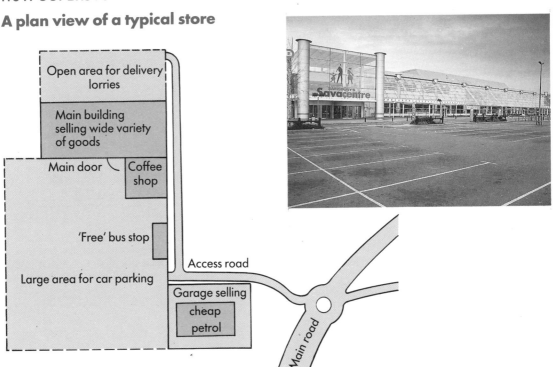

Open area for delivery lorries

Main building selling wide variety of goods

Main door

Coffee shop

'Free' bus stop

Large area for car parking

Access road

Garage selling cheap petrol

Main road

ACTION!

Look carefully at the plan and the photograph above.

1 What attractions are there for the motorist?

2 Why should deliveries only take place at the back of the store?

3 Do you have to own a car to use this store? Why?

4 Give two reasons why being next to a main road is very important for the store.

Why industry comes and goes

Case study: The iron and steel story in South Wales

In 1861 During the 19th century iron and steel works grew up on the South Wales Coalfield where iron ore, limestone and coal were found. These are the '**raw materials**' for iron and steel production. They are very heavy products that are difficult and expensive to transport. It was much easier and cheaper to make iron and steel close to the raw material.

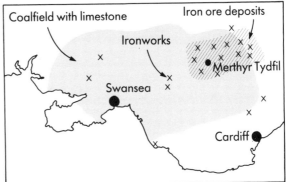

Coalfield with limestone

Iron ore deposits

Ironworks

Merthyr Tydfil

Swansea

Cardiff

There used to be many small ironworks (35 in all), each producing small quantities of iron.

In 1991 Nowadays, steelworks are found on the coast. This is because the iron ore (in Wales) is expensive to mine and the best quality ore has already been used. It is now cheaper to import iron ore from abroad. It is still heavy and expensive to transport, so a location near to a port is best.

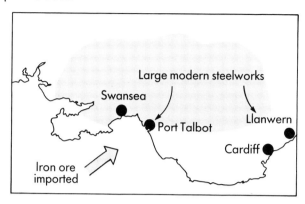

Today there are only two large, modern steelworks using the most advanced technology to produce steel.

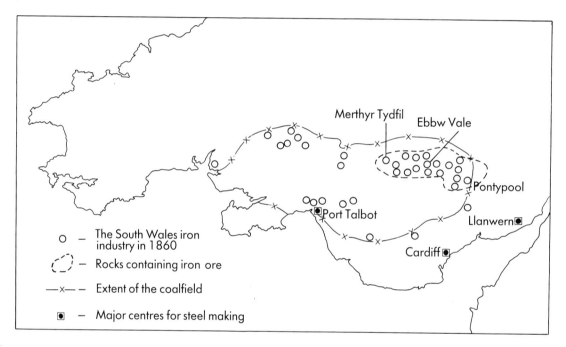

ACTION!

1 Give two reasons why ironworks were located 'on the coalfields' in 1861.

2 What is meant by the term 'raw materials'?

3 Give two reasons why steelworks are located on the coast nowadays.

4 Why do you think there are only two steelworks operating now in South Wales?

Why economic activities develop in particular locations

Case study: The M4, South Wales

- Nowadays people and goods have to be able to travel quickly so the land next to motorway junctions has become very desirable.

- As farming is becoming less profitable, some farmers are looking to sell off their land to the highest bidder.

A variety of economic activities has sprung up between junctions 33 and 35 of the M4.

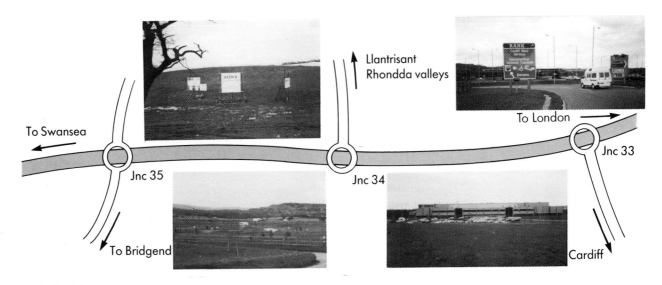

To Swansea ← Jnc 35 — Jnc 34 — Jnc 33

↑ Llantrisant Rhondda valleys

To London →

To Bridgend ↓

Cardiff ↓

ACTION!

What are the advantages for each of the above economic activities at this location?

LEISURE AND THE LAND

Each year nearly 100 million people visit the **National Parks** of England and Wales. The National Parks are areas of 'outstanding natural beauty' which were identified by an Act of Parliament in the 1950s for special protection and public enjoyment. Although the name 'National Park' suggests they belong to the nation, this is not the case. Most land is privately owned and is for many of the owners their livelihood.

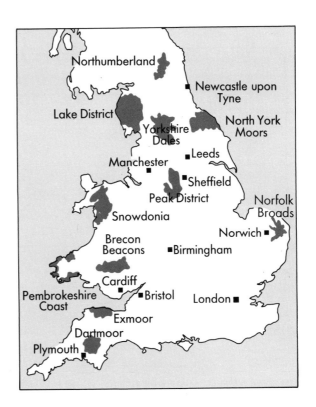

Problems in the countryside?

The very visitors for whom National Parks were set up to be enjoyed can cause great damage – most of the time without realising it. The worst problem is that most visitors come at the same time, e.g. a warm Sunday afternoon during the summer.

Landowners need to use the land to make a living, but there are rules about what the land can be used for. Building is strictly controlled.

Visitor
I want to be able to walk across the fields. I need somewhere to stay. I need picnic areas and toilets. I need somewhere to park my car. I want to be able to drive around the National Park and go wherever I please!

Landowner
I need to use modern farming methods to make a decent living. I don't want tourists tramping over my land, leaving gates open, dropping litter and letting their dogs scare my animals.

National Park officer
I have to make sure the rules are followed. The natural beauty of the park must be preserved and the general public must be able to enjoy it. I have to meet local needs regarding development, small scale industry and agriculture. Visitors must have car parks, toilets and information centres. I also encourage volunteer groups to do conservation work.

Villager
My village is full of cars in the summer so there is too much noise and exhaust fumes. My son cannot afford to buy a house because city people push the price up. I can't even build an extension or have the double glazing I want.

(represents the National Park Authority)

Start anywhere on the left-hand side of this grid and see how quickly you can get across.

NPA	The committee that controls the Parks	G	Don't leave these open
NPO	The representative of the NPA	CW	You can volunteer for this!
LO	80 per cent of Exmoor belongs to them	FaB	For tourists on 2 legs or 4!
V	100 million each year in National Parks	L	Don't drop it – take it home
B	Strictly controlled in National Parks	EF	Too many cars cause this pollution
CP	Self-catering tourists stay here	PS	Eat your lunch here
C	Pitch your tent here	H	Not enough of these for local people
D	Town on Exmoor	SaC	Exmoor farmers rear these
HaC	They wear away footpaths		
CC	Rules of the countryside		

Grid (hexagons):

H — L — PS
FaB — V
SaC — LO — CW
NPO — EF
CP — CC — G
HaC — C
NPA — B — D

Let's look at Exmoor

More than 80 per cent of the 265 square miles of Exmoor is privately owned. Most of it is used for farming, especially sheep and beef cattle. The public has great freedom within Exmoor, as there are over 600 miles of footpath and bridleways. This freedom is because of the tolerance of the landowners – so long as the visitors respect the Countryside Code.

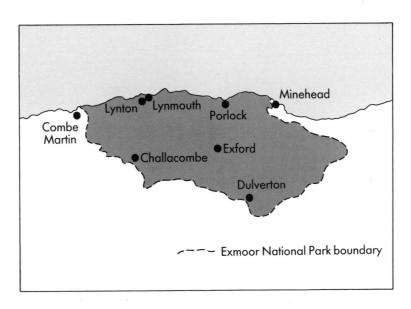

Lynton · Lynmouth · Porlock · Minehead · Combe Martin · Challacombe · Exford · Dulverton

– – – Exmoor National Park boundary

Problems! – on Exmoor?

- Farmers enclose land – 1/7th is ploughed up or fenced off.
- Hikers and climbers wear away footpaths.
- Shortage of houses for local people – they can't afford to pay the high prices like those who come from the city.
- More tourists prefer to self-cater, so they need more caravan parks and campsites.
- More cars means that more land has to be used for car parks.
- More visitors means more noise, more litter, more traffic jams and more of a danger to wildlife.

Exmoor's Changing Face

Many visitors tend to have a romanticised view of the countryside and of the people who live there. But as any countryside dweller will tell you, it isn't always like that.

Here on Exmoor the cost of living has all but caught up with the rest of the UK. The same cannot be said of the local wages. Employment prospects have always been thin, in or out of recession, and for years many local youngsters have looked elsewhere for their future.

It is true that, nowadays, there are more jobs in tourism than in agriculture, but most are seasonal and unlikely to provide for full family support.

The influx of better-off people from away – usually to retire – affects the price of housing and thus the prospects of the local first-time homemaker. Shops, schools, health and recreation are becoming more centralised in the towns – the village school and shop are now rarities in the remoter communities – and public transport has become confined to the busier routes on the fringes of Exmoor.

Urban influences tend to prevail; and, as elsewhere, television is inevitably diluting the local culture.

The backbone of Exmoor's community still remains those who shape its landscape – the farmers and the landowners. Despite mechanisation, their work is no less hard than their ancestors'. But profit margins are low or non-existent and survival has been largely dependent on hill farming support grants. Now, with subsidies being constantly eroded, many Exmoor farmers face difficult times ahead.

(From: The Exmoor Visitor, March 1991)

UNIT 15
Using the Earth's resources

NATURAL RESOURCES

The Earth is rich in natural resources. These are the things that are found within or on the Earth that can be used by mankind. Natural resources can be grown on the land; caught in the sea; reared by farmers; mined or quarried. Natural resources differ from **manufactured goods** because manufactured goods are made in a factory from **raw materials.** Natural resources can be divided into two types:

Non-renewable   These are resources that can be used only once. Once they have gone, they have gone forever.

Renewable   These are resources that will not run out, provided they are not over-exploited.

People have become very concerned of late about how quickly we are using up the Earth's non-renewable resources. Many may run out (become **exhausted**) soon into the next century. Although new **reserves** are found every day, sometimes they are not enough to cope with excessive use.

Resource	Runs out in
Diamonds	2008
Silver	2010
Gold	2018
Oil	2025
Zinc	2028
Tin	2030
Lead	2036
Copper	2044

One way of prolonging the life of non-renewable resources is by **recycling**. Britain is way behind some of its European neighbours when it comes to recycling. Nevertheless, the number of bottle banks and paper recycling centres is increasing and people are gradually becoming more aware of recycling potential.

Product	Amount recycled in 1990
Steel	60%
Copper	40%
Aluminium	35%
Paper	33%
Glass	10%
Plastic	8%
Rubber	6%

ACTION!

1 Are the following products renewable or non-renewable?
coal   wheat   fish   cotton   timber   iron ore

2 Explain what is meant by the following words in geography:
exhausted   reserves   recycling   resources   manufactured goods   raw material

3 Match the correct manufactured item with its raw materials:

Raw material	Manufactured items
Cod	Wooden table
Iron ore	House brick
Gold	Railway rail
Wool	Fish finger
Timber	Sweater
Clay	Wedding ring

4 Construct a bar graph using the figures in the 'runs out in ' table (see previous page).

HOW EXTRACTING NATURAL RESOURCES CAN DAMAGE THE ENVIRONMENT

Case study: Coal

Coal is one of Britain's most important natural resources. It was coal that gave Britain the power to develop its other resources during the Industrial Revolution.

A hundred years ago, when coal mining was at its height, very little attention was paid to the environment. It was the coal that was important and any waste was simply dumped close to the mines. As more coal was mined, more waste was dumped, until huge coal tips or spoil heaps could be seen. Today the coal mining areas of Britain are scarred with these ugly remnants of past mining. Opencast mining causes even more damage.

How coal tips damage the environment

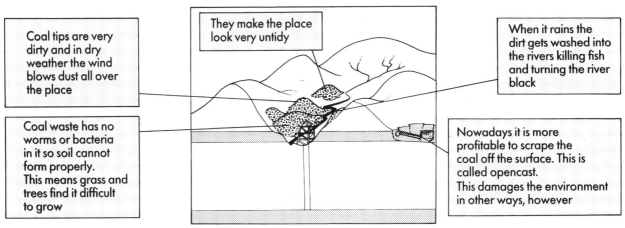

Coal tips are very dirty and in dry weather the wind blows dust all over the place

Coal waste has no worms or bacteria in it so soil cannot form properly. This means grass and trees find it difficult to grow

They make the place look very untidy

When it rains the dirt gets washed into the rivers killing fish and turning the river black

Nowadays it is more profitable to scrape the coal off the surface. This is called opencast. This damages the environment in other ways, however

Can damaged landscapes be restored?

Once an environment has been polluted it is very difficult to put it back to what it was before. It can be done, but it involves a lot of money, time, effort and a will to want to do it.

In some coal mining areas efforts are being made to 'reclaim' old coal tips.

This involves:

1 Clearing the tip using heavy machinery. Modern technology means that some of the coal that was dumped can now be burnt in our more efficient power stations.

2 Landscaping the area. This involves bulldozers putting the land back to its original shape.

3 Fertilising the area and introducing worms and bacteria to help the soil form.

4 Spreading grass seed over the whole area.

ACTION!

Improving the environment can be done on a very small scale. It does not have to involve a lot of time or expense. All it needs is a little bit of effort. For example, litter could be collected from a park or the school grounds.

1 Design an activity to improve a small part of your local environment.

2 Get a group of friends to help you carry out the task.

3 After you have completed it, ask yourself 'Have I really improved the environment?'

4 Think of ways to stop the problem occurring again.

ENERGY RESOURCES: IF THE PRICE IS RIGHT!

Case study : Oil in Alaska

Oil is an example of a non-renewable fossil fuel. That means it was formed many millions of years ago and once gone, it will never return. The developed world has become increasingly dependent on oil and as it becomes more scarce governments and oil companies are prepared to go anywhere in the world to search for it. As more oil is used, its price goes up and the desire to produce more increases. Eventually, through improvements in technology, it becomes 'economically feasible' to exploit known oil reserves even in the most inhospitable parts of the world.

The facts
- Alaska is the northernmost state of the USA.
- The USA needed oil.
- In 1965, oil was found in vast amounts in Prudhoe Bay.
- There was a six-year delay on the pipeline decision mainly because of environmental concerns.
- In 1977 the pipeline was completed.
- Reserves should last for 50 years.

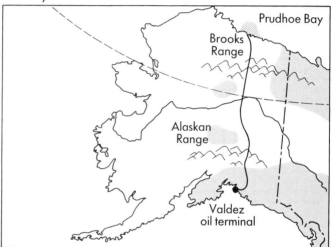

The problems
- Oil was found in the north but was needed 4000 km to the south.
- Prudhoe Bay is frozen for 10 months of the year – difficult for tankers.
- Temperatures fall to –50° C in winter, often with blizzards.
- The ground is permanently frozen, making mining and building difficult.
- Workers don't want to live in such a difficult environment thousands of miles from their families.
- Parts of Alaska are mountainous and prone to earthquakes.

The solution
Build a pipeline 1285km long from Prudhoe Bay in the north to Valdez in the south, overland for most of the way, to carry 1.2 million barrels of warm oil every day!

ACTION!

1 What is meant by the term 'economically feasible'?

2 List some of the problems engineers had to overcome when building the pipeline.

3 How do you think oil companies attracted people to work in such a difficult environment?

What has Alaskan oil meant for the local people and the environment?

– Represented a physical barrier to migrating caribou. Underpasses had to be built

– Built on stilts so the warm oil would not melt the frozen ground

– Alaska is home to a wide variety of bird life

– 600 streams and rivers had to be crossed – including spawning ground for salmon

The plight of the Eskimo

Most Eskimos now no longer live in the traditional manner – hunting whales and seals and living 'on the ice' in igloos. Most Eskimos are now fully integrated into a 'westernised' culture. Eskimos now live in permanent settlements, eat western-style diets and many of them have jobs in the oil industry. The outside world came to Alaska and changed the traditional society, some say not for the better.

What happens when it all goes wrong?

Case study: The Exxon Valdez

The fragile environment of Alaska can be easily upset. This was tragically demonstrated on March 24 1989, Good Friday, when the oil tanker *Exxon Valdez* spilled 11 million gallons of crude oil into Prince William Sound. The tanker had just loaded up in Valdez

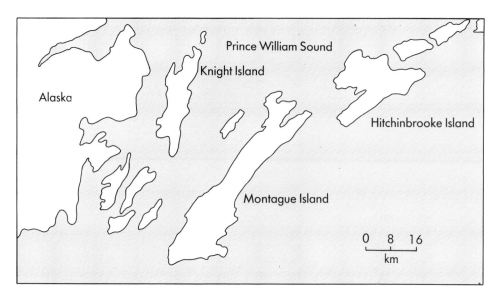

and was en route for California. Soon after midnight on that fateful day, whilst trying to navigate through Prince William Sound, it hit rocks and was holed below its water line. They said it would never happen – but it did. The ecological tragedy Alaska had been waiting for had finally happened.

Why was it so bad?

– Prince William Sound is sheltered. That means it only has small waves. These do not break up the oil as well as large, powerful waves. The oil could remain for years.
– This rocky coastline has many bays and coves. The total area affected was 800 miles.
– A 30 mph wind hampered the clean-up operation and caused the oil slick to travel further down Prince William Sound.
– There was a seven-hour delay in the rescue barge carrying the clean-up equipment. This meant more oil spilled into the sea.

One victim of the oil spill

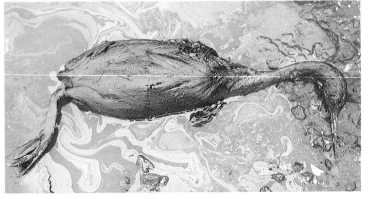

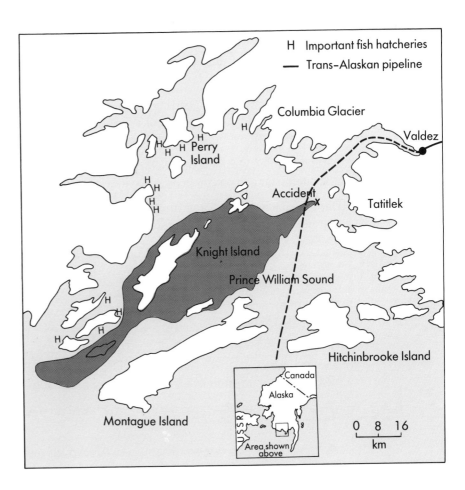

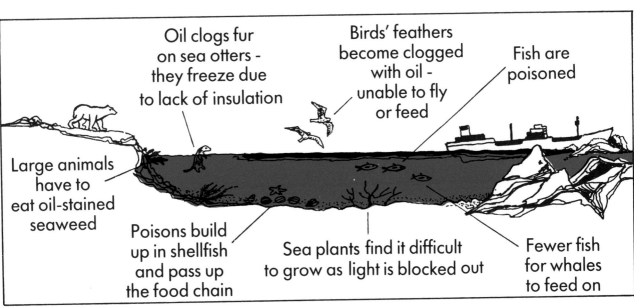

Spill Could Hit Alaska Wildlife for 10 years
by Roger Highfield, Science Editor

It could take 10 years for the Prince William Sound area to recover completely from the Alaskan oil spill disaster, experts said yesterday.

Exxon is assembling a team of marine biologists to evaluate the effects of the spill.

Facilities have been set up to treat oiled birds and mammals, such as otters, bears – which like to forage on the beach – and seals. Exxon is also working with local fishing interests to help identify and protect the most sensitive areas.

The body count is not what matters in calculations of the effect of the spill on the area. The crucial factor is the percentage of the local stock of each species that has been killed.

The season, speed of reproduction and movement of species from unaffected areas govern the recovery cycle.

Sea otters, migrating birds, herring and salmon are likely victims of the spill, according to one conservative group, the Defenders of Wildlife. The Sound is home to more than 20 000 sea otters, hundreds of sea lions and some killer whales.

Mr Rupert Cutler, president of the conservation group, said oil could destroy the insulating ability of the otters' fur and poison them when they eat oil-soaked fish.

'If the oil remains on the sea and the beaches for two more weeks, it could also kill millions of ducks, geese and shore birds which migrate through Prince William Sound.' Mr Cutler said.

ACTION!

Read the newspaper article above.

1 Name:
   (a) Two fish
   (b) Three birds
   (c) Two other creatures which have been affected by the spill.

2 What will happen if sea otters' fur becomes soaked in oil?

3 Use your knowledge to explain why it will take ten years for the area's wildlife to recover.

4 In your opinion is it worth going to Alaska for oil? Give reasons for your answer.

Are there any alternatives to fossil fuels?

Case study: Tidal power in the Severn estuary

Geothermal power

Wind power

Solar power

ALTERNATIVE ENERGY SOURCES

Tidal power

Biomass and dung

Hydro-electric power

Nuclear power

Using the power of the tides is a popular alternative source of energy. It works in this way:

• A barrier is built across the estuary.
• The barrier has gates which open and close along its length.

- The incoming or outgoing tide drives turbines as it flows through the gates.
- The turbines produce electricity.

In order for a tidal power station to produce sufficient energy there must be a big difference between high and low tides – this is called the **tidal range**.

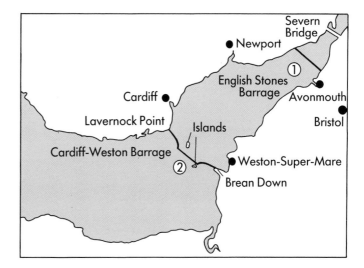

The Severn Estuary has the second largest tidal range in the world. The shape of the estuary is ideal. As the tide rushes in and out it is 'funnelled' so the energy is concentrated. After a 'feasibility study' by the Severn Tidal Power Group, two schemes were put forward:

1 a smaller English Stones barrage near Avonmouth;

2 a much larger barrage stretching from Cardiff to Weston.

The second scheme has been recommended.

How it works:
- Sluice gates open when the tide is coming in.
- They close when high tide is reached so water is trapped behind the barrage.

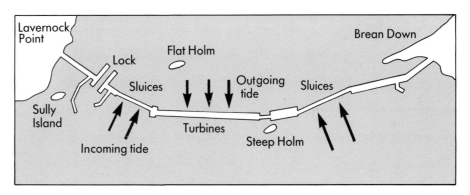

- At low tide, sluice gates close. Turbines open to the water rushing through, which generates electricity.
- Ships would be allowed to pass through special locks.

Advantages of the scheme:
- Cheaper, reliable electricity.
- Bristol Channel dangerous for leisure activities at the moment – barrage would make it safer.
- Many jobs created for builders, engineers and power station staff.
- Popular tourist attraction.
- More fish and birds in the quiet waters above the barrage.
- No harmful gases released into the atmosphere.

Disadvantages of the scheme:
- It will cost £6000 million to build.
- Industrial waste and sewage presently dumped in the estuary would need costly treatment.
- Power stations already using the estuary for cooling would have to change their systems.
- Rivers Usk and Wye are important for salmon – the barrage would threaten these.
- Mudflats along the estuary are important for wading birds – these would be threatened if barrage was built.
- Ecological balance would be upset.

ANSWERS

Unit 1

The British Isles: page 9
1 (a) London (b) Bristol (c) Belfast
2 (a) C3 (b) C3 (c) C4
3 C3
4 Newcastle
5 West
6 Cardiff
7 South East, London
8 Southampton, Bristol/Cardiff, Leeds

Physical map of Britain: page 10

North Sea
Cotswolds/North Sea
River Exe/English Channel
River Severn/Cambrian Mountains
Pennines/North Sea
River Shannon

Harder activity
1 Scottish Highlands: Ben Nevis, 1343m
Southern Uplands: Merrick, 843m
Pennines: Cross Fell, 893m
Lake District: Scafell, 978m
Cambrian Mountains: Snowdon, 1085m
Exmoor: Dunkery Beacon, 520m
Dartmoor: High Willhays Tor, 618m

2 Mersey: Derbyshire; Irish Sea. Clyde: Southern
Uplands; Firth of Clyde. Tyne: Northumberland;
North Sea

3 Shetlands; Orkneys; Scilly Isles; Outer Hebrides;
Inner Hebrides; Channel Islands

What is a map? page 11

Tim leaves his house in Brook Street and turns right into
Bailey Road. He crosses the road near the park. At the
next junction, he turns left into Church Street. He walks
down Church Street, passing the Dog and Duck pub
and the church on his left and the public telephone on
the other side of the road. At the traffic lights he turns
left into Mary Street, crosses the road and visits the
library. When he comes out of the library he turns left
towards the traffic lights. At the junction he turns left
into Church Street and heads towards the garage. At
the junction he crosses the road to the grocery store,
turns right and heads towards John's house on
Hawthorn Hill.

Measuring distance: page 14

(a) 2km (b) 1½km (c) ¾km (d) 6km (e) 2½km
(f) 4½km (g) 700m (h) 400m (i) 550m

Grid references: page 15

1 (a) Raleston (b) St. Harry (c) Short Park
(d) Horse bridge

2 (a) 0423 (b) 0420 (c) 0121 (d) 0124

3 (a) Church/Post Office/Houses (b) School/Post
Office/Houses

4 (a) Farmhouse (b) Clubhouse (c) Farmhouse

Grid references: page 16

⚑	Golf course	095145
⬦	Glasshouse	114144
✚	Church with steeple	084160
CH	Clubhouse	092153
☼	Viewpoint	104155
▪	Church with tower	116175
△	Triangulation pillar	117158
⚚	Windpump	088168
⚔	Battlefield	094175
P	Post office	109162

Height on maps: page 17

2 A: Less than 10m   B: 20m   C: 30m
D: Between 30 and 38m

Cross-sections: page 20

2 9399: steep 9597: flat 9394: gentle

Following a route on a map: the Treasure Hunt: pages 20–21

1 (a) 43m (b) Whitley Batts (c) Chelwood Bridge
2 (a) East (b) Post Office and church with tower
3 (a) Park Farm (b) Hunstrete Plantation
4 (a) Uphill (b) South
5 31m
6 (a) right, then right again (b) 10km

Graphs: page 22

1 Pie chart 2 Scattergram 3 Line graph 4 Bar graph

Unit 2

Stephen's street: page 24

1 16 **2** Ael-y-Bryn **3** No. Only residents and their visitors

Living in the country: page 27

1 Open spaces; away from pollution and noise; walking

2 Not being able to see friends often; relying on her parents; no-one of her own age around

3 Advantages: very little crime or vandalism; fresh air; open spaces; no traffic; pleasant surroundings; more privacy

4 Disadvantages: few public services, e.g. buses and trains; having to travel some distance to doctor, dentist, shops, cinema, etc

Living in the city: page 28

1 Being near friends and leisure activities

2 The crowds; the traffic; pollution; noise; crime

3 (a) Andrew does not rely on his parents so much to drive him around. He can meet his friends regularly after school
(b) Both are very active and enjoy sport and going to the cinema with friends

Unit 3

The European Community: page 29

1 1: Republic of Ireland 2: Portugal 3: France
4: Germany 5: Denmark

2 B: Berlin C: Copenhagen D: Dublin
L: London P: Paris

3 Athens; Madrid; Brussels

4 Twelve

Italy: page 30

1 1: Tyrrhenian Sea 2: Adriatic Sea
3: Mediterranean Sea

2 A: Sardinia; B: Sicily

3 C: Cagliari; F: Florence; P: Palermo; T: Turin;
V: Venice

4 The Arno; The Tiber

5 The Apennines

North Italy: page 32

1 Able to sell products; closer to main markets; cuts down on transport costs

2 Power from water – need fast-flowing mountain streams

South Italy: page 33

Social
New schools, etc
Piped water, etc
Malarial marshes drained

Industrial
Laws, etc
85% Grants available, etc
New dams, etc
Smaller farms, etc
New port facilities
Hotels built, etc

Agricultural
Farmers, etc
Forests planted, etc

France: page 34

1 1: English Channel 2: Bay of Biscay
3: Mediterranean

2 Corsica

3 Bordeaux, Lyons, Marseilles, Nantes

4 The Seine and the Rhone

5 I: Alps; II: Pyrenees; III: Massif Central

Contrasts in France: page 36

1 (a) Paris *or* French Riviera; (b) Massif Central

2 Brittany: history, culture, beaches
Massif Central: mountain scenery
Paris: sights, shops
Alps: scenery, walks, mountains, winter sports
French Riviera: Mediterranean, sun, sea, beaches, climate
South-West: climate, beaches

Paris: page 37

1 It was a defensive site

2 (a) Government centre, roads and railways meet there, TV and radio centre, universities, industrial centre

3 1 Encourage more cars to be used, so increasing noise and fumes
2 Would not really discourage people, as many do not mind paying fines
3 Would create more congestion as people look for parking spaces
4 Very drastic – would reduce economic activity

Massif Central: page 38

1 Primitive, backward, poor soils, steep slopes, harsh climate

2 Highland area with steep slopes. No work to attract people

3 (a) No jobs: no facilities for young; hard life
(b) Bright lights, discos, bars, better housing, job prospects

4 Maintain the economy, maintain culture, they do not want mass migration

5 Only occupied by owners during holiday period – little money stays in area. Local house prices forced up

Tourism in the European Community: page 39

1 Travel agents, tour operator, coach driver, pilot, air steward/ess, courier, waitress, bar staff, etc

4 Portugal, Spain, France, Italy, Greece, Yugoslavia. Attractions of the Mediterranean and its climate

5 Too cold

Holidays in Britain: page 40

1 Fine beaches; warmer, drier summers

2 Centre of British tradition; many sights to see; theatres

3 Families. All-round entertainment – something to do on wet days

4 Any (give valid reasons)

Holidays in the sun: page 43

1 Mediterranean/Aegean

2 Beaches; climate; traditional Greek food; culture

4 Electricity; jobs provided; hotels built; marina built; new roads built, marshes drained

Winter resorts: page 44

1 Winter resorts are increasing in popularity

2 (a) An activity that needs special training, equipment and facilities (b) A prepared area for skiing (c) Evening entertainment

3 (a) It is guaranteed to have snow (b) Skiers need snow!

4 Deforestation; compact soil; ski lifts use up land; many people are attracted to an environmentally sensitive area – pressure on scarce resources

Unit 4

Atlas skills 1: physical features of the world: page 45

4 (a) Murray/Darling; Zambezi; Limpopo; Orange; Parana; Plate; Sao Francisco, etc, (b) Andes

5 An imaginary line in the Pacific Ocean; when crossed a day is either gained or lost

Economic development across the world: page 47

2 (a) Italy (better food; hygiene; medicines. More doctors per person)
(b) Few doctors; poverty; few hospitals

(c) Able to learn new skills; education increases chances of getting jobs

Developed and developing countries: page 49

Developed country
Few employed in agriculture
Factories use machines, etc
Many employed tertiary, etc
Farming advanced, etc
Factory workers work for set time, etc
Developing country
Many employed in agriculture
Factories need a lot of workers
Fewer employed in tertiary sector, etc
Farming very primitive, etc
Factory workers work long hours, etc

British employment structure: page 43

2 More services; machinery used in primary and manufacturing industries; industry and farming are more efficient

Bangladesh: page 50

1 (a) 1: Nepal   2: India   3: Burma   4: Bhutan   5: China (b) Bay of Bengal (c) Tropic of Cancer: $23\frac{1}{2}°N$

2 Many mouths to feed; problems may worsen in future; children need looking after

3 They are poor and must produce their own food. They cannot buy it and have no chance of other employment

Bangladeshi family: page 53

1 (a) Father: farming, feeding oxen (b) Mother: cooking; washing up; looking after children; gathering firewood (c) Children: farming, firewood, washing clothes

2 The local stream

3 'The oxen are fed and watered'

4 Firewood

Natural hazards: page 54

1 It brings fertile mud and silt

2 A tropical storm

3 Water funnels up the Bay of Bengal, increasing the wave height

4 Low-lying land; no warnings; primitive houses; lots of people in one small area; no medical facilities

Brazil: page 55

1 (a) 1: French Guiana; 2: Surinam; 3: Guyana; 4: Venezuela; 5: Colombia; 6: Bolivia; 7: Paraguay; 8: Argentina; 9: Uruguay; 10: Peru   (b) A: Pacific Ocean; B: Atlantic Ocean   (c) C: Equator; D: Tropic of Capricorn

2 Too young to work; need to be looked after; difficult to control population in future

3 Dense jungle, inaccessible

Life in Brazil 1: page 57

1 (In order) First paragraph: superb, businessman; coffee; exports; parties; drunk. Second paragraph: struggle; his best; shack; overcrowded; water; proper

2 SE first; NE second

3 1: High class; 2: Low class/poverty line

4 There is tremendous wealth in Brazil but at the moment it is not distributed equally throughout the country

A typical Indian village: page 59

1 (a) 5   (b) 2   (c) 1   (d) 7   (e) 3   (f) 4   (g) 6   (h) 8   (i) 9

2 Wood: spears; bow and arrows; blowpipe; dugout; housing frame. Grasses/reeds: fishing nets; roof; hammock

Changes in the Amazon rainforest: page 61

1 Dense forest
2 Deforestation; settlers moved in for agriculture and industry; roads built; land cleared
3 Road enables large machinery to be brought in
4 Need to bring in supplies of food
5 From farming and timber

Japan: page 64

1 (a) Hokkaido; Honshu; Kyushu; Shikoku   (b) Asia (c) Tokyo

2 Cassette players, CDs, TVs, videos, video cameras, cameras

3 (b) Electrical goods, cameras, cars, etc

4 The need to import raw materials; mountainous interior

5 Commitment to work; workers are loyal to company; determination to succeed, etc

Imports and exports: page 65

1 Imports: goods brought into a country. Exports: goods sold to other countries   Balance of trade: the difference between imports and exports   Manufactured goods: things made in a factory

2 Foodstuffs; tea and coffee; fuels and minerals; chemicals

3 (a) Middle East; Indonesia   (b) Japanese goods need lots of oil in their production

5 Countries gain wealth; some countries have goods which are not found elsewhere

Unit 5

Earthquake in Mexico: page 69

1 It happened during a 'rush hour'

2 Buildings collapsed, gas mains exploded, services were cut off

3 No light or water, no fuel, further tremors

4 The streets were covered in debris

5 500 miles (804.672km)

6 It is built on stable rock

Mount St. Helen's: page 71

2 An area once renowned for its scenic beauty is now a wasteland

3 A bulge appeared on the side of the mountain; gas escaped from the volcano; there had been an earthquake

4 People are attracted to 'disaster areas' – it is now a famous mountain

Plates: page 72

2 They are close to plate boundaries

3 Britain is not near a plate boundary. It is in a stable part of the world

Unit 6

Hydrological cycle: page 74

1 Ocean   **2** Plants   **3** Groundwater
4 Atmosphere   **5** Snow and ice
6 Rivers and lakes
A: Precipitation;   B: Transpiration;
C: Condensation;   D: Throughflow;   E: Run off;
F: Evaporation

The river story: page 75

1 Exmoor   **2** B: Tiverton C: Exeter   **3** Culm
4 English Channel   **5** South

Hydrographs: page 80

1 A: Gentle rising limb; rural area; permeable rock
B: Steep rising limb; urban area; impermeable rock

2 B: because the peak flow is higher than in A

Unit 7

Reservoirs: page 83

1 (a) Chairman   (b) Local resident   (c) Water Company Manager   (d) Conservationist (e) Farmer   (f) Watersports enthusiast

2 For: chairman, water company manager, watersports enthusiast   Against: farmer, local resident, conservationist

3 Narrow valleys are easy to dam; deep, so they hold a lot of water; mountains have few people and heavy rainfall

4 Water meters; public awareness; 'Save it' campaigns; advertisements; water-efficient appliances

Dirty water: page 83
(In order) Acid rain; Sewage disposal; Nitrates; Landfill seepage; Factory discharges; Power stations; Traffic fumes

North Sea: page 85
2 England, Scotland, Norway, Denmark, Germany, The Netherlands, Belgium, France

Unit 8

River processes: page 91
1 Loose material; a gentle slope gradually built up above river level

2 By its brown colour

3 Steep banks; undercutting

Coastal photograph: pages 96–7
1 It is exposed to the elements

2 It came from further along the coast, was transported by longshore drift and deposited where the waves lose energy

3 To keep the beach stable

4 Their edges are knocked off by attrition and corrasion

5 There are more cracks in cliffs, and waves frequently wash in and out

Sketch map of Devon coast: page 98–99
1 Prevailing winds blow directly onto the coast; the Atlantic Ocean has large waves

2 It is an exposed point; ships are blown onto rocks in storms

3 By being cut back

Westward Ho!: page 100
1 (c) South-west

2 River flowing into the sea

3 By wave action from the sea

Erosion: page 101
1 Waves strike the coastline directly; soft rock

2 The map shows the coastline during Roman times

3 Very hard rock breaks up wave energy

4 (a) Costs of protection are not as high as costs of the consequences
(b) Protection costs are less than the cost of building new homes, new roads, etc

5 Bays would develop further south, attracting tourists

6 (a) There is such a wide area to cover
(b) Erosion will always occur – all we can do is slow it down

Unit 9

Weather and climate: page 103
1 (a) Windy conditions bring dangerous waves
(b) Storms at sea can threaten boats
(c) Frosts may kill young, tender plants
(d) People do not shop as much in bad weather

Microclimates: page 103
1 1: 24°C   2: 26°C   3: 18.4°C   4: 22°C   5: 21°C

2 (a) site 2; (b) site 3

3 Site 3

4 Site 1 is quite warm, due to its tarmac playground; 2 is sheltered from the wind, so is warm; 3 is exposed to the cooling breeze; 4 is sheltered by trees; 5 is not in the shade and is on a grassy surface

Weather in Britain: page 105
1 (a) False (b) True (c) True (d) False

2 W: Blackpool; X: Pembroke; Y: Inverness; Z: Bournemouth

3 (a) During July temperatures decrease south to north. Coleraine is further north, so cooler. During January temperatures decrease west to east, away from the influence of the Atlantic Ocean. Coleraine is closer to the warmer ocean
(b) It is more inland and furthest south, so quickly warms up
(c) A huge curve around the Irish Sea – the sea is warmer than the land

High pressure: page 107
1 Similarities: clear skies; sunshine. Differences: very cold, foggy in winter

2 Wind strength and direction

Low pressure: page 108
1 A warm front passing over

2 The move from cold to warm to cold sectors of the depression

3 It moves anticlockwise around a depression – as the depression moves, the wind direction changes

Weather vs. climate: page 109
4 About average – this is shown by the same amount of blue and red on the graph

Climate change: page 112
2 Do not use cars so much; use energy more efficiently; use paper wisely, so trees are not unnecessarily cut down; recycle as much waste as possible

Unit 10

Vegetation: page 114

1 Rainforest: dense, green, tall, variety of species; Grasslands: tall grass, few trees; Deserts: very sparse, little vegetation

2 Look at: amount of rainfall; distribution of rainfall; temperature; seasons

3 Heavier rain areas have more vegetation

The rainforests: page 115

1 (a) True (b) False (c) False (d) False (e) True

2 Undergrowth: vegetation on the floor of the forest; Lianas: creeper-like plants; Epiphytes: plants which grow on other plants; Parasites: things which feed on other living things

3 For stability, and to transport nutrients to the top of the tree

4 (a) They make good furniture (b) Ebony, mahogany and teak

Savannah: page 116

1 Savannah has a long, dry season

2 They have thick outer skins; they store water

3 The change is related to the amounts of rainfall

Deserts: page 117

Desert plants are… competition for water
Clouds are not… descending air creates high pressure
During the night… temperatures fall rapidly
Growth rates in… plants need to conserve water
The main limiting… the lack of water
Plants can produce… don't know when the rains, etc

Unit 11

Egypt: population: page 119

1 57 people per square km

2 Sparse, except near the River Nile

3 They are all in one area

4 Mountainous; desert

5 Near water supply, lowland; the river means food can be grown

Birth and death rates: pages 119–20

3 (a) 1921; (b) It would decrease

4 Differences: higher birth and death rates; greater total population; greater rate of natural increase in Bangladesh. Similarities: population increasing; death rates fell initially

Population change: page 121

Little change; rapid increase; rapid decrease

Size of families: page 121

1 Children are expensive to bring up; women want to pursue careers; family planning, etc

2 They help produce food; it is the custom; they will look after parents when they are older, etc

3 It is low in developing countries

Reasons for moving: page 122

A forced move: fear of persecution; famine; disease; war; possibly promotion

Choice: new house; friends and relatives; marriage; retirement; attractive areas; possibly promotion

Ernie Martin: page 123

2 (a) Five (b) Three

Kurds page 124

3 War

4 Lack of food; cold; poor hygienic conditions; exhaustion, etc

5 Threat of losing their lives

Unit 12

Settlements: page 126

2 Dry point: B; Gap: C; Defensive site: D; Wet point: A; Bridging point: E

3 E: all roads should lead there; D: Defensive reasons

Settlement patterns: page 128

1 Nucleated: C; Dispersed: B; Linear: A

2 The crossroads

3 It is confined by a narrow valley

4 Farmers

Town functions: page 129–30

1 A, B and C: Industry; D: Administration centre; E: Port; F: Market centre; G: Resort

2 (a) B (b) C (c) A

3 D: All roads lead there; it is easier to get to

4 G: It is a tourist area

5 F: It is a farming community

6 D: Need to be near roads; it is the largest settlement, with more people

Minehead: page 133

1 (a) More housing; better trade possibilities – more tourists; an eyesore disappears
(b) Yes! Increased tourist traffic in summer, but who will benefit – local traders or the holiday company?

Cardiff Bay: page 137

1 Danger to wildlife; flooding; break up of communities; water quality

2 It will clean up the area; clean the rivers; if not here, then other environments would be destroyed

Unit 13

Transport: page 139

(In order) Car; bus; pipeline; air; air; rail

Too much traffic!: page 141

2 Description of line graph: Peaks during rush hours when many people going to and from work. Little during early hours

Are there solutions?: page 143

More: 1, 3, 5, 8, 10 Less: 2, 4, 6, 7, 9

Where to build a by-pass: page 144

1 1: Goes through farmland

  2: Golf course affected

  3: Hills and woods affected

2 Route 2 is better – it is shorter and would affect a smaller area than the other suggested routes

Channel Tunnel: page 146

1 For: building worker; chairwoman; people with holiday homes; businessman. Against: steward; farmer; villager; customs officer

Unit 14

Competition for land: page 147

1 Large: farm; golf course; airport; industrial complex; motorway. Small: sports centre; house; shoe shop

2 Building a housing estate; building a link road

Can the rate of soil erosion be reduced?: page 149

1: E; 2:D; 3:C; 4:A; 5:F; 6:B

Mr Meadmore's Farm: page 151

1 Cheese; milk; butter; yoghurt, etc

2 Too far for them to walk

3 (a) Growing a different crop in each field every year

  (b) It allows fields to regain their fertility

Shoe shops: page 152

1 Shop 1: it is closest to the car park

2 No: you like to compare prices and styles

3 Shop 5: it is furthest from the car park

Superstores: page 153

1 Cheap petrol; easy parking

2 Lorries need large areas to turn – they do not disturb shoppers this way

3 No: there is a free bus service

4 Easy access for customers and deliveries

Industry in South Wales: page 154

1 They needed coal and iron ore from the local area, and a supply of limestone

2 The products which go to make something in a factory

3 The need to import raw materials; cheap land available

4 Very expensive to run a steelworks; fall in demand for steel products

South Wales: page 155

All are near a motorway for transport services and near major towns for workforce needs

The Earth's resources: page 160

1 Renewable: fish, timber, wheat, cotton; Non-renewable: coal, iron ore

2 Exhausted: run out; Reserves: what is left in the earth; Recycling: using each product more than once; Resources: valuable materials; Manufactured item: something that is made; Raw materials: things needed to make something

3 Cod: fish finger; Iron ore: rail; Gold: ring; Wool: sweater; Timber: table; Clay: brick

Oil in Alaska: page 162

1 More profit is made than costs incurred

2 Frozen ground; wildlife; darkness; severe cold

3 High wages; holiday benefits

Alaskan wildlife: page 166

1 (a) Herring, salmon (b) Ducks, geese, shore birds (c) Otters, bears, seals

2 They will freeze to death

3 Fragile environment; very harsh climate, etc

GLOSSARY

Abrasion A form of erosion where rocks rub against other rocks.

Accessibility How easy a place is to get to.

Acid rain Rainwater mixed with gases produced when fossil fuels are burnt.

Agriculture Farming the land and producing food.

Algal bloom Large amounts of algae found in the sea.

Aluvium Fertile mud spread by a river during flood.

Alternative energy Energy resources other than fossil fuels.

Amenities Places of relaxation and enjoyment.

Antarctic Circle An imaginary line around the Earth at a latitude of 66½°S.

Anticyclone A high pressure weather system.

Arable farming The growing of crops.

Arctic Circle An imaginary line around the Earth at a latitude of 66½°N.

Ash Material that comes out of a volcano during an eruption.

Assembly plant A factory where lots of different parts are put together to make a finished product.

Atlas A book containing maps of the world.

Atmosphere The gases that surround the Earth.

Attrition A form of erosion where two rock particles rub together.

Balance of trade The difference between imports and exports.

Barrage An artificial wall built across a bay or a river.

Base flow The usual amount of water flowing in a river.

Bay An inlet found at the coast.

Beach Sand or pebbles deposited along a coast.

Biological weathering The breakdown of rocks by plants and animals.

Birth rate The number of people being born per year.

Blowhole A hole on a cliff above the sea, from which air escapes.

Bore hole A hole dug deep into the ground.

Bridging point The easiest place to build a bridge across a river.

Business park A collection of businesses and factories in one place.

Buttress A large root found in trees in the rainforest.

By-pass A road built around a town.

Canopy The continuous layer of tops of trees found in the rainforest.

Capital The amount of money needed for any venture.

Capital city Usually the most important city in a country – where the centre of government is found.

Cavitation Erosion caused by bubbles in fast-flowing streams.

Central business district The commercial centre of the town.

Channel The part of the land in which a river is found.

Chemical weathering The breakdown of rocks by acids in rainwater.

City A large town with many services.

Cliff A steep or sheer rock face.

Climate The average weather of a particular place.

Cold front Where cold air meets warmer air.

Commercial The buying and selling of goods or services.

Communications The ease with which people and goods can move from place to place.

Community A group living together.

Comparison goods Goods where people can compare prices and styles.

Composite cone A volcano made up of alternate layers of ash and lava.

Condensation Water droplets as a result of a drop in temperature.

Congestion A build-up of traffic, usually in a town.

Conservation Looking after the environment.

Continent A large land mass made up of a number of countries.

Contour line A line joining places of the same height above sea level.

Contour pattern Groups of contour lines showing the shape of the land.

Convectional rainfall Rainfall caused through warm air rising from a warm surface.

Corrasion Erosion caused by pebbles rubbing against solid rock.

Corrosion Erosion resulting from chemical change.

Country The land that is run by a particular government.

County A small part of a country.

Course The path a river takes.

Crop rotation Growing different crops in the same field each year.

Cross-section A way of showing the shape of the land.

Dairy farming Producing milk and milk products.

Dam A wall built to keep back water.

Death rate The number of people who die per year.

Defensive site The place chosen for a settlement that is easy to protect from attack.

Derelict land Wasteground which was once built on.

Deposition The gradual build up of pebbles, sand and small particles of rock.

Depression A low pressure weather system.

Developed country A wealthy country which has developed its resources.

Developing country A poor country which is trying to develop its resources.

Direction Shown on a map by a compass.

Discharge The amount of water in a river.

Drought A long period without rainfall.

Earthquake A violent shaking of the Earth's crust.

Eastings Shown on a map as the vertical lines of a grid.

Economic output The total amount of goods coming out of a factory or a country.

Economically viable Where the profits made are greater than the costs incurred.

Emigrant A person who moves away from a town or country.

Emergents The largest trees of the forest.

Employment The number of people who have jobs.

Environment The places where people live.

Epicentre The point on the Earth's surface where an earthquake occurs.

Epiphyte One plant growing on another plant.

Equator An imaginary line around the Earth at latitude 0°.

Erosion The natural wearing away of rocks.

Eruption When a volcano throws out rock, ash, lava and gas.

European Community A group of twelve European countries.

Evaporation Water changing from a liquid to a gas as a result of being warmed.

Exports Goods being sold to other countries.

Factory A building where things are made.

Farm A piece of land where crops are grown or animals are kept for food.

Farming Producing food on a farm.

Fertile soil A soil which is good for growing things in.

Fertiliser Substances that help crops to grow.

Fetch How far a wave has travelled.

Fieldwork Gathering data outside the classroom.

Finished product A complete article from a factory that can now be sold.

Flood Water covering land that is usually dry.

Flood plain The flat area of land next to a river.

Flood risk Whether or not it is likely that a flood will occur.

Fossil fuels Fuels that are burnt e.g., gas, coal and oil.

Focus The exact point within the Earth where an earthquake takes place.

Freeze-thaw action Repeated freezing and thawing.

Freight Goods that are being transported from one place to another.

Fresh water Water, found on the land, that is not salty.

Frontal rainfall Rain occurring as a result of warm air meeting cold air.

Function The main purpose of a town.

Gap town A town formed between two hills.

Glacier A river of ice.

Goods Items that people use.

Gorge A very steep-sided valley.

Grants Money given by the government for a specific purpose.

Greenhouse effect The heat from the Earth not allowed to escape back into space.

Grid Lines on a map.

Grid reference A way of finding places on a map quickly and accurately.

Gross national product The total value of all goods and services produced by a country in a year.

Groundwater Water that exists within the rocks of the ground.

Groyne A wall on a beach built at right angles to the sea.

Hamlet A small village.

Headland A rocky piece of land sticking out into the sea.

Hierarchy Shops grouped together according to size and importance.

High pressure A weather system usually bringing clear skies.

High water mark The level reached by high tide.

Home market Goods produced for, and sold in, this country.

Home region The area in which you live.

Housing estate A collection of modern houses.

Humus Dead and decaying leaves and other parts of plants.

Hydraulic action A form of erosion where water squeezes air into cracks.

Hydro-electric power Power generated by using water.

Hydrograph A graph showing the relationship between the amount of rainfall and the amount of water in a river.

Hydrological cycle The path water takes from the sea, to air, to land, to sea.

Ice sheet A large expanse of ice found in high latitudes.

Immigrant Someone who has moved into a town or city from another country.

Impermeable Something through which water will not pass.

Imports Goods brought into a country from abroad.

Income How much a person or a country earns.

Industry The term used to describe the production of goods and the generation of wealth.

Industrial estate An area of land where several factories can be found.

Infant mortality The number of babies who die before their first birthday.

Infertile soil Soil that is no good for growing crops.

Inner city The old industrial area next to the city centre.

Interlocking spurs Fingers of land around which a river winds itself.

International Date Line An imaginary line at about 180° of longitude. Every time you cross it the date changes.

International trade The exchange of goods and services between the countries of the world.

Irrigation The moving of water to grow crops.

Island An area of land surrounded by water.

Isobar A line joining places of the same pressure.

Isotherm A line joining places of the same average temperature.

Key Usually found on a map, a line of symbols and their meanings.

Lag A time delay.

Landfall sites Huge holes in the ground where domestic rubbish is dumped.

Latitude Imaginary, parallel lines running from east to west across the Earth.

Lava Rock which comes out of a volcano.

Leeward The side of a hill facing away from the wind.

Leisure Spare time.

Ley grass Grass that is planted.

Lianas Long, thin, rapidly growing plants found in the rainforest.

Life expectancy How long people are expected to live.

Linear A straight line pattern.

Literacy rates How many people can read and write.

Load The amount of rocky material in a river.

Local area The area surrounding your house or school.

Longitude Imaginary lines running around the Earth from the North Pole to the South Pole.

Long shore drift The way in which pebbles and sand are moved along the coast by the sea.

Low pressure A weather system that usually brings cloud and rain.

Low water mark The level of low tide.

Magma Collective name for all material thrown out by a volcano.

Magma chamber Where magma is stored before a volcanic eruption.

Manufactured goods Products that are made in factories.

Manufacturing Making things in a factory.

Map A drawing of a place or area.

Market The place where goods are sold.

Meander A large bend in a river.

Microclimate The weather of a very small area.

Migrant Someone who has moved home.

Migration The act of moving home.

Mixed farming Farming that grows crops and keeps animals.

Mouth Where a river ends.

National park A protected area of outstanding natural beauty.

National Rivers Authority The organisation that has responsibility for keeping rivers clean.

Natural features Not man-made.

Natural hazard A natural threat to life, e.g. volcano, earthquake or flood.

Natural increase A population term used to describe the difference between birth rates and death rates.

Natural resources Things of value found in nature.

Network A series of roads or railways linked together.

Non-renewable resources Resources that will run out one day.

Northings Shown on a map as the horizontal lines of a grid.

Notch A small area at the base of a cliff eroded by the sea.

Nucleated Centred around one place.

Ocean A large expanse of sea.

Ordnance Survey The organisation that produces Ordnance Survey maps.

Organic farming Farming without using artificial chemicals and fertilisers.

Organic material Plant and animal remains.

Overhang The part of a waterfall that will eventually collapse.

Parasites Plants and insects that feed on other living organisms.

Parent material The original rock from which a soil forms.

Passengers People who are travelling.

Pastoral farming The farming of animals.

Permanent pasture Grassland that is never ploughed up.

Permeable Something through which water passes easily.

Petro-chemicals Chemicals produced from oil.

Physical map A map showing natural features, such as mountains and rivers.

Physical weathering The breakdown of rocks into smaller and smaller particles.

Pie graph A circular graph, usually used to show percentages.

Plan view A view from directly above.

Plain A flat piece of land.

Plate A solid section of the Earth's crust.

Plate tectonics The study of how the Earth's plates move.

Political map A map showing countries, counties, towns and cities.

Pollution Things that can harm the environment, e.g. chemicals, dirt and noise.

Population The total number of people in an area.

Population density The number of people living in a specific area.

Port Where goods are brought into and sent out of the country.

Poverty Very low standards of living.

Precipitation All water which falls from the sky as rain, snow, hail, etc.

Prevailing wind The direction from which the wind normally blows.

Primary activity The extraction of natural resources.

Prime meridian An imaginary line of longitude 0°, running through Greenwich, from the North Pole to the South pole.

Questionnaire A list of questions designed to ask people their opinions on a subject.

Rainforest The dense, jungle lands of the world.

Rain shadow An area which does not receive much rain, due to being protected by a mountain.

Ratio The proportion of one variable to another.

Reclaimed land An area of land which was once under the sea.

Recreation A pleasurable interest or activity enjoyed during spare time.

Recycling Using products more than once.

Redevelopment Modernising areas of land that have become derelict.

Region An area of a country.

Relief The shape of the land.

Relief rainfall Rainfall found on mountains where air is forced to rise.

Renewable resources Resources that will never run out.

Reserves A supply of resources which could be used in the future.

Reservoir An area of stored water.

Resident Someone who lives in an area.

Resort A town that specialises in providing holidays.

Resources Things that are useful to mankind.

Richter scale A scale used to measure earthquake intensity.

Ridge A long, narrow hill.

Route The path taken on a journey.

Run off Water moving across the Earth's surface.

Rural In the countryside.

Saltation A way in which small particles jump downstream.

Salt marsh An area of land where sea water becomes stagnant.

Sanitation Related to the disposal of human waste.

Savannah Large areas of grassland.

Scale The link between the distance measured on a map and its true distance in reality.

Secondary activity The making of goods in a factory – same as manufacturing.

Seismograph An instrument used to show the intensity of an earthquake.

Services An economic activity where nothing is produced, but a person's skill is paid for.

Settlement A collection of buildings where people live.

Sewage sludge Produced by human waste.

Shock waves A series of tremors occurring after an earthquake.

Silage Grass that is cut green, sealed and kept for winter feed.

Silt Small particles of mud found in a river.

Site The place where a town or a factory is located.

Sketch map A rough drawing of a place.

Slurry Farmyard waste.

Social conditions People's standard of living.

Soil erosion The washing away of the soil.

Soil texture The size of the particles making up the soil.

Solar radiation Heat and light received from the sun.

Solution Chemicals that are dissolved in water.

Source The start of a stream.

Spit A pebble or sand deposit found along the coastline.

Spot height The height of a specific place as shown on a map.

Stack A piece of rock found along the coast where erosion is occurring.

Storm flow The extra amount of water in a river as a result of a storm.

Storm surge The extra height of the high tide as a result of a storm.

Stream A small river.

Suburbs The residential areas found on the the edge of a town or city.

Succulents Plants that are adapted to living in desert conditions by storing water.

Superstore A large shop selling most household items and food.

Suspension Material held within the main body of a river.

Tertiary activity Providing services

Throughflow Water flowing through the soil and rocks.

Tidal range The difference between the highest and lowest tides.

Tidal wave A huge wave resulting from a storm or an earthquake.

Tourist Someone who visits an area for recreational purposes.

Town A large collection of buildings.

Traction Material being rolled along the bed of a river.

Transpiration Water given off by plants.

Transport The movement of people, goods and other materials from one place to another.

Treatment works Where domestic water supplies are cleaned.

Tributary A small river joining a larger one.

Tropic of Cancer An imaginary line of latitude at 23½°N.

Tropic of Capricorn An imaginary line of latitude at 23½°S.

Tsunami A tidal wave.

Tube well A way of obtaining water in dry countries.

Typhoon A tropical storm.

Undercutting Erosion eating away at the base of a cliff.

Undergrowth Vegetation lying on the surface under the tree layer.

Urban Towns and cities.

Urbanisation The rapid growth of towns and cities.

Valley The low ground between two hills.

Vegetation The plants of an area.

Village A small settlement.

Volcanic eruptions Periods when a volcano is giving off steam, lava, gas and solid particles.

Warm front A place where warm air is forced to rise above colder air.

Water cycle The ways water moves, from the sea, to the air, to the land, and back to the sea.

Waterfall A point in a river where water falls vertically for a distance.

Wave-cut platform A flat area of coastline where cliffs have been eroded.

Wave refraction The bending of waves in the sea.

Weathering The breakdown of rocks by the weather.

Weather satellite A piece of machinery in space which sends information about the Earth's atmosphere.

Wind The movement of air.

Windward The side of the mountain directly facing the wind.

World Bank The organisation to which poor countries apply for loans.

Yield How much is produced from a set area of land.

Index